That'll Preach!

That'll Preach!

5 Simple Steps to Your Best Sermon Ever

Charley Reeb

Abingdon Press
Nashville

THAT'LL PREACH:
5 SIMPLE STEPS TO YOUR BEST SERMON EVER

This book is printed on acid-free paper.

Library of Congress Cataloging-in-Publication Data has been requested.

ISBN: 978-1-5018-3547-6

Unless otherwise indicated, all scripture quotations are from the Common English Bible. Copyright © 2011 by the Common English Bible. All rights reserved. Used by permission. www.CommonEnglishBible.com.

Scripture quotations marked (KJV) are from The Authorized (King James) Version. Rights in the Authorized Version in the United Kingdom are vested in the Crown. Reproduced by permission of the Crown's patentee, Cambridge University Press.

Scripture quotations marked (NIV) are taken from the Holy Bible, New International Version®, NIV®. Copyright © 1973, 1978, 1984, 2011 by Biblica, Inc.™ Used by permission of Zondervan. All rights reserved worldwide. www.zondervan.com. The "NIV" and "New International Version" are trademarks registered in the United States Patent and Trademark Office by Biblica, Inc.™

17 18 19 20 21 22 23 24 25 26—10 9 8 7 6 5 4 3 2 1
MANUFACTURED IN THE UNITED STATES OF AMERICA

In memory of William L. Self,
who taught me that the greatest of these is preaching.

There is not now nor has there ever been an acceptable substitute for Christian preaching.
—Paul Scherer, *The Word God Sent*

If Protestantism ever dies with a dagger in its back, the dagger will be the Protestant sermon.
—Donald Miller, *The Way to Biblical Preaching*

The power of a sermon lies in its structure, not in its decoration.
—Halford E. Luccock, *In the Minister's Workshop*

Contents

Contents

Preface

I know what you might be thinking: "Five simple steps to my best sermon ever? Really?" Maybe you've read your fair share of books on preaching and have never seen such a bold claim. I imagine most of the preaching books you've read are edifying but not very easy to apply. I'm also guessing most of those books have not produced results for your preaching ministry. This book is not only easy to apply but will equip you to preach the best sermons of your life.

This is not a textbook. There are plenty of those. This is a practical book born out of more than twenty years of preaching in the local church and over fifteen years teaching the practice of preaching. In the following pages you will discover a secret to great preaching. More importantly, you will learn to apply the secret in five simple steps and experience astonishing results. When you finish reading this book your only disappointment will be that it was not available to you sooner.

Whether you are an experienced pastor, youth minister, seminary student, or lay speaker this book will take your preaching to the next level. You are about to learn how to communicate the gospel in a way that transforms lives and a have a lot of fun doing it! This book will also be useful to anyone who speaks publicly in any capacity.

Warning: do not skip ahead to the five steps. I know it is tempting, but the method will be revealed to you soon. Absorbing the ideas before it is crucial to applying the five steps for maximum impact.

Introduction

Congratulations! You are about to discover the secret to great preaching. It is not a secret because no one is aware of it. It is a secret because many preachers know it but ignore it, much to the suffering of their ministry. Sadly, the secret to great preaching is hidden in plain sight. I am willing to bet you have come across it but dismissed it because you thought it was too simple. Now that you have this book in your hands you are one sermon away from being a better preacher. You will apply the secret and marvel at the fruits of your preaching. What you are about to learn could revolutionize your ministry. Everything you need to preach with confidence and power can be found in the following pages.

This book is practical and gives you a method and a framework to deliver dynamic and inspiring sermons every time you get up to preach. Sound unrealistic? Just keep reading and give it a shot. I imagine you want your preaching ministry to improve and have the kind of results you had hoped for but have not yet achieved.

I am sure you work very hard on your sermons. You grind over the biblical text and dig deep into your faithful commentaries. You spend much time in prayer. You have a burning conviction in your soul to reach people with the gospel, but your messages are not having the impact you desire. Perhaps you see your listeners yawn, check the time, and text their friends while you are preaching your heart out. Maybe you are tired of working so hard with little to show for it. Something needs to change but you don't know how to change.

It is said that the definition of *insanity* is doing the same thing over and over again expecting different results. It's time to try something new. It's time to do something that really works! All of the great preachers you admire use this secret. You can be great too if you simply apply it.

You may be thinking, "OK, who is this guy? How does he know this so-called secret, and why should I believe him?" Preaching is my first love. I believe with all my heart that faithful preaching changes lives. I have been preaching the gospel in local churches of all sizes for over twenty years. Presently I serve as senior pastor of one of the largest churches in the Florida conference of The United Methodist Church. While serving the local church, I spent several years studying homiletics (the craft of preaching) at the graduate level, earning a doctor of ministry in preaching. I am an instructor of preaching to local pastors in course of study programs. I also serve on the proclamation team of my conference's board of ordained ministry and work with pastors seeking to improve their preaching. In all my time preaching, studying preaching, and teaching preaching one thing has become clear: there is a secret to great preaching. Those who apply it become great preachers. Those who don't apply it struggle with preaching effectively. It's that simple.

Let's get one thing out of the way. The secret to great preaching is not prayer. I know that is common advice, and it sounds good but don't believe it. A faithful prayer life is vital to effective preaching, but prayer alone will not make you a great preacher. I know some of the most spiritually devoted ministers who struggle with preaching. The truth is you can pray harder than a monk, be wiser than a desert father, and know scripture better than your Bible professors and still not have a great preaching ministry. If you want to be a preacher who is consistently used by God to change lives you must apply the secret.

The secret is not original with me. I have simply observed and applied what all great communicators of the gospel do. I have used the secret in my sermons for years and continue to marvel at the results. I have taught the secret to many preachers and they are always amazed at how transformative it is for them and their listeners. You will be too!

Are you ready to look at your finished sermon and say, "That'll preach!" and walk to the pulpit with confidence? I imagine your next opportunity to preach is right around the corner. You can apply the secret immediately and preach your best sermon ever. Let's get started!

Chapter One

The Problem and the Solution

If you are unhappy with the results of your preaching it is probably not your fault. Chances are you went to a seminary (or currently attend one) that was great at teaching you how to interpret the Bible. Your professors were probably excellent at helping you discover the nuance of a biblical text and the original meaning of the Hebrew and Greek words of the Bible. Most seminaries are fantastic at equipping preachers to be interpreters of scripture.

But here is the problem. Most seminaries are ineffective at equipping preachers to communicate to average listeners in a local church. In fact, many seminaries hardly attempt to teach preachers how to be effective communicators. The seminary I graduated from was superb in many ways, but they only required one introductory preaching class. If you wanted to learn more about how to become an effective preacher, you had to rearrange your schedule and take elective courses when they were available. Unfortunately, my experience is not the exception. Many seminaries only require one introductory preaching class to graduate with a master of divinity. That's hardly enough training in a discipline that is paramount to the role of a local pastor.

Unless seminary students grew up in churches with good preachers, their professors have the biggest influence on their preaching. Many seminary professors have little-to-no ministry experience in the local church. This includes preaching professors. They are far removed from the texture of parish ministry and generally preach to those in the academic world. So it follows that many seminary students get the wrong impression about what it takes to preach effectively "in the field." A highbrow sermon may stir those in a seminary chapel but it will not work in the trenches of a local church.

Over the last forty years inductive preaching has become very popular in mainline seminaries. The impact of preaching revolutionary Fred Craddock and the rise of the "new homiletic" has led to a variety of inductive and narrative preaching styles. This style of preaching is known for turning "three points and a poem" upside down. Instead of beginning with the main idea of the scripture text and breaking it down into specific ideas, an inductive sermon begins with specific ideas and questions and concludes with a main idea. Quite often inductive sermons arrive at "open-ended" conclusions so listeners can draw their own conclusions about the message. This is a noble thought, but it's not realistic for most listeners.

There is a great deal to learn from inductive preaching. The sermons are clever and imaginative but the style and message are typically lost on average listeners. Novelty sometimes sacrifices clarity. Unless you have a congregation filled with preachers and seminary professors a steady diet of inductive preaching is not effective in most local churches. Most preachers don't have the time to create such novel art every week. More importantly, most listeners don't have the patience to sit through it. Listeners keep asking, "Is there a point?"

What I have discovered as I have taught other preachers is that many of them prepare sermons designed to reach the crowd at a seminary chapel service. They imagine their seminary professors sitting in the back pew critiquing their sermons. They have been rigorous in their research of the biblical text. They are diligent in communicating exegetical material. They quote biblical scholars and theologians to demonstrate their education. Basically, their sermons sound like a "research dump." Other preachers sound like they have just come from a creative writing retreat. They have read everything Barbara Brown Taylor and Fred Craddock have written and seek to imitate what cannot be duplicated or appreciated by most listeners.

If you are preaching every week to other preachers and professors, stick with this approach. However, if it is your goal to reach the majority of listeners in churches you must change your approach. You will never become an effective preacher looking over your shoulder for your seminary professors. If you want the gospel to connect with real people who have real needs in real life you must apply the secret. Am I saying to forget what seminary taught you? Absolutely not! All of your knowledge must be reframed in a way that connects with your listeners. With that in mind, let me tell you a secret.

The Secret

So what is the secret to great preaching? It is three simple words: **Engage your listeners!** You know, those people you are talking to in worship—the ones who chose not to do a thousand other things on a weekend so they might hear a relevant word from God for their lives. Let me repeat that: engage your listeners! Stick those words on your computer. Put them in your Bible. Type them on the top of your sermon notes. Write them on a card and put them on the dashboard of your car. Get a tattoo that says it . . . well, just kidding. You get my point.

I know. Looks too simple, doesn't it? To tell you the truth it is deceptively simple. Many preachers ignore the secret by assuming their listeners will be engaged regardless of what they say and how they say it. This is a fatal mistake, and it's the mentality of preachers who have difficulty connecting with their listeners.

This may sting a little but if you want to be a great preacher you must accept it: "If people aren't interested they're not listening."[1] The great pulpiteer J. Wallace Hamilton said that quote over fifty years ago. If it was true then, it is especially true today. If your listeners are not interested in what you have to say they are not going to pay attention to you. Oh, they may look like they're listening but their minds and hearts are far away. They are thinking about the talk they must have with their bosses on Monday, their grocery lists, where they are going to lunch after worship, or the texts they have received that look more interesting than anything you are saying. They have checked out and the opportunity for them to be transformed by your message has been lost.

So how do you get your listeners interested in what you have to say? Engage them! And how do you engage them? To begin with, stop thinking about your seminary textbooks, commentaries, and professors, and start thinking about the lives of your listeners. To be blunt: Don't be selfish when you prepare sermons. Think of others when you preach! Ask yourself, how will this biblical message engage those who take the time to get up, dress up, and show up to worship?

When you preach there may be a woman sitting in the back who is going through a bitter divorce. There may be a teenager who has been dragged to worship by his parents. He is texting his friends and can't wait to get out of there. There may be a man sitting near the front who hasn't been to church in years because of how harshly he was treated by his Christian friends. He is giving it another try. There may be a college student who scurried in late to the service. She grew up in the church, but now she is questioning her faith. There may be a nervous mother in attendance whose baby is in the nursery for the first time. You may also have a young family checking you out. They have just moved into your neighborhood and are looking for a church home. How will your sermon connect with each of these people? Will it connect? Be honest. Will they remember what you said thirty minutes after worship?

Here is a good exercise. If you are currently serving a church, spend ten minutes writing down everything you know about your people, both good and bad. If you are not serving a church make the same list about your family and friends—health issues, peer pressures, questions of faith, marital problems, graduations, family problems, issues with kids, issues at work, births, deaths, personal struggles and temptations, new jobs, job layoffs, money problems, great achievements in sports, and so on.

When you are finished with the list, take a good look at it and ask yourself this question, "Have any of my sermons in the last few months touched on most of these experiences?" Now ask yourself this question, "What difference do my sermons make for people who are going through these experiences?" And then ask yourself a third question, "Why should the people on the list care about the messages I preach?" Finally, ask yourself, "Is it easy for the folks on this list to understand my sermons?"

The Curse of Knowledge

The previous exercise exposes whether or not you are connecting with your listeners. Many preachers are plagued with something that often becomes an obstacle to engaging listeners. It is called "the curse of knowledge."[2] Chip and Dan Heath use this phrase in their book *Made to Stick* to describe the greatest obstacle for any communicator: making the assumption that your listeners know as much as you about your subject or will process and understand your message like you. In other words, you assume your listeners have your frame of reference.

Have you ever heard really boring speakers and asked yourself, "Are they aware of how boring they are?" Perhaps you were amazed that they continued to drone on completely unaware that their listeners were bored stiff. Why does that happen? Well, when those speakers prepared their speeches they assumed their listeners would hear and understand the subject with their frame of reference. They were as happy as can be giving the speech thinking, "Yes, this is great. This has to be great because if I were listening to a speech on this subject this is exactly what I would like to hear!" These speakers are typically dumbfounded when they find out their listeners were less than impressed. It never occurred to them that their listeners didn't have the same experience with their subject matter.

The hard truth is that the same thing often happens in worship services every weekend. Preachers preach sermons they would love to hear, and that's the problem! Most listeners don't share the same frame of reference as their preachers. However, many preachers don't recognize this important fact, or they ignore it. When listeners don't connect with a message, preachers don't blame themselves—they blame their listeners. These preachers will whine, "My congregation just doesn't have ears to hear. They are shallow people. I'm casting my pearls before swine. If I had a more spiritually receptive congregation they would appreciate my sermons." The truth is their listeners would be very receptive to their messages if their preachers made the effort to engage them. Instead, some sermons might as well be lectures on computer programming. The listener is thinking, "Preacher, what are you trying to say and what difference does it make in my life?"

Speaking the Language

I can hear those voices in the back of your head asking, "Isn't this suggestion just pandering to the crowd and entertaining them? And where does the Holy Spirit come into play in all of this? Isn't preaching the gospel enough? Why should I have to work so hard to be heard?"

First, engaging your listeners is not pandering to them or entertaining them; it's respecting them and caring about them. When you engage your listeners you are showing sensitivity to where they are in their lives and offering something that could help them. Average listeners today don't care what you have to say if they don't sense that you understand them and care about them. Jesus knew this, which is why he was such an outstanding communicator. The Bible says of Jesus, "The large crowd listened to him with delight" (Mark 12:37). Why? Because he engaged them. He walked among them, listening to them, caring for them, and healing them. He told stories and illustrated his messages with everyday examples they could understand. Jesus's listeners knew he cared, which is why they probably hung on his every word. Jesus was figuratively and literally "the Word . . . made flesh" (John 1:14 KJV).

Second, the Holy Spirit plays a critical role in helping you engage your listeners. In fact, given what occurred on the day of Pentecost we can be certain the Holy Spirit desperately wants the gospel spoken in a language everyone can understand. Read the story in Acts 2. When the Holy Spirit came upon the church everyone heard the gospel "in their native languages" (Acts 2:6). I believe that is what preachers are called by God to do: communicate the gospel in a language people can understand, to allow the word to become "flesh" for them. In other words, engage your listeners!

Third, if you think preaching engaging sermons is some new-fangled idea or product of a watered-down church culture, read these words of John Wesley about his own preaching: "I labour to avoid all words which are . . . not used in common life; and in particular those kinds of technical terms that so frequently occur in bodies of divinity."[3]

If you read Wesley's sermons you will observe that he knew his audience. He realized he was not preaching primarily to seminary students and professors or "bodies of divinity." His sermons were heard and read by people from all walks of life, which is why he often described his preaching as "plain truth for plain people."[4] He addressed relevant issues of average people in his time and context. Wesley's sermons may seem pedantic to us today, but for his time Wesley was a very engaging preacher. He was intentional about preparing sermons that were accessible to his listeners.

Finally, to those who believe preaching the gospel should not require any extra effort to engage listeners, why have a sermon at all? Why not just read a text of scripture and then give the benediction? If sermons don't need to engage listeners to be heard, reading scripture should suffice, right?

We all know that is not enough. If we are to penetrate the lives of our listeners with the word of God we must interpret scripture and proclaim the gospel for our time and context. This requires using the tools of effective communication. The Bible itself contains various rhetorical devices and other persuasive strategies. Biblical writers were inspired by God to engage people, and they used their gifts as communicators to do it. When we engage listeners we are simply taking our cue from biblical writers.

We must be as prepared as we can be as communicators of the gospel. Don't our sermons deserve our very best? Of course we must allow the spirit of God to work through us. We are channels, not the source. But some channels are more prepared than others. God communicates through us best when we have done our part. As Augustine is attributed as saying, "Without God, we cannot; without us, God will not."

Before I show you the five steps to great preaching you must understand the essential characteristics of engaging sermons. This is vitally important. You can't apply the five steps without them. So turn to the next chapter. I have a "point" I want to make.

Remember

- The secret to great preaching is to engage your listeners.

- "If people aren't interested they are not listening."[5]

- Avoid the "curse of knowledge" by never assuming your listeners have your frame of reference.[6]

- Preaching is making the "word become flesh" for your listeners.

And Your Point Is?

One of my favorite comedies is *Planes, Trains and Automobiles* with Steve Martin and the late John Candy. Martin plays Neal Page, an uptight business man trying to get home to his family for Thanksgiving. His flight home is delayed because of the weather. This delay begins a chain of hilarious traveling fiascos that will have you laughing until you cry. A huge part of the hilarity is Del Griffith, an obnoxious and chatty travel companion played by Candy, who Neal gets stuck with along the way. Del is a real blabbermouth. He talks incessantly, which bugs the daylights out of Neal. Finally, Neal can't take it anymore. He blows a gasket and shouts something to Del that every preacher should commit to memory: "You know, everything is not an anecdote. You have to discriminate. You choose things that are funny or mildly amusing or interesting. You're a miracle! Your stories have none of that! . . . Here's a good idea. Have a point. It makes it so much more interesting for the listener!"[1]

It is funny, but like all good humor there is much truth in it. In the case of preaching it is painfully true. In fact, preachers should have this quote engraved, framed, and prominently displayed on their desks. Neal's rant names one of the most prevalent problems in sermons that do not engage listeners: lack of focus. Some preachers don't "discriminate" and put too much information in their sermons, and a lot of it is not funny, mildly amusing, or interesting. Most importantly, all this vast information often lacks focus, which makes it very uninteresting for the listener.

When I began my ministry my problem was that my sermons had too many ideas and illustrations. They lacked focus and development. I mistakenly thought that in order to keep people interested in my sermons I had to fill them with as many clever points, insights, and stories as possible. Those poor people! Thankfully, a sarcastic remark from a wise lady in my church taught me otherwise. I had just preached what I thought was a pretty good sermon. It was chock full of points, quotes, and anecdotes. As I was shaking hands with people leaving worship, the lady approached me with a slight grin on her face. I was looking forward to hearing the wonderful things she might say about my sermon (Come on, you know you've done the same thing!). Instead, she shook my hand and quipped, "Nice sermon series." Those three words turned out to be one of the greatest lessons I ever learned about preaching: less is more.

In those early days of ministry I am sure many of my sermons sounded like commercials for an upcoming sermon series. They weren't bad, but there was no substantial development of an idea or enough focus to keep my listeners on track. Worst of all, I wasted a bunch of valuable material that could have made up several good sermons.

When I lead workshops and classes on preaching I find many sermons are plagued with the same problem. They are flooded with ideas, points, stories, and anecdotes that cause a lack of focus and development. I understand why because I used to make the same mistake. The thought is, "I'm going to impress the heck out of them and give them a bunch of great material!" The end result is usually a "hodgepodge" of content that confuses and overwhelms listeners. We need to take the advice a veteran journalist gave a preacher: "There's no sense saying more if it means they'll hear less."[2]

I remember hearing a sermon that covered every idea in Christendom. I was so amazed and amused at the cornucopia of subjects the preacher mentioned that I wrote them all down. He talked about Christ and redemption, the kingdom of God, peace and social justice, prevenient and justifying grace, heaven and the second coming, and the sacrament of communion. Oh, and he even threw in the power of prayer for good measure! It was like he thought he was going to drop dead as soon as he left the pulpit, so he wanted to preach about everything he could before he left the earth. Well, I am all for the idea of preaching each sermon as if it were your last, but if your sermons are fire hoses of information that lack focus one day your listeners will pray for your last sermon!

The truth is listening is hard work, which is why so few people do it. The average listener is not going to work very hard listening to a sermon, especially one that is confusing and lacks focus. I am not talking about your saint of an uncle who hasn't missed Sunday worship in thirty years or your grandmother who said, "You can always get something out of every sermon if you listen hard enough." I am talking about average listeners who show up to worship every six weeks if they don't have any better offers and leave early to beat everyone to lunch. The burden is on you to keep them engaged. If they have difficulty tracking your sermon they will stop listening to you and may never come back to your church.

While writing this book I asked a worshipper what he looked for in a sermon. His reply was, "Pastor, I appreciate that you keep me awake." Now you can scoff at what he said but that is where many of your listeners are coming from. Does that mean your job is to entertain them by making your sermon a shallow spectacle? No, but it does mean you must simplify your sermons so they are easy to follow. If your sermons are not clear and easy to follow, your listeners will start playing tic-tac-toe on the back of an offering envelope and begin passing the gum. There is an old saying in preaching: "A mist in the pulpit is a fog in the pew."[3] What that means is that if you are a little unclear about the focus of your sermon the lack of clarity will be magnified to your listeners. You know what they say: "If you aim at nothing, you are sure to hit it!"

Sermons are like taking people on a trip. The great preacher Clovis Chappell used to say, "A good sermon needs to be like a journey: we begin, we travel, we arrive."[4] There must be a sense of movement and direction in every sermon. Sermons filled with too many points and ideas often lack focus, progress, and development. Listeners must feel the sermon is going somewhere or they will not take the trip. As my wise preacher friend Riley Short likes to say, "Sermons should not have conclusions; they should have destinations."

Have a Point!

Let me get to the point: **For razor sharp focus prepare your sermon around one compelling and clear point.** Now, hold on. I am not suggesting that having a sermon with one point is the only way to maintain focus. There are many wonderful preachers who preach very effective sermons with more than one point. I am suggesting that it is much easier for listeners to stay focused on a sermon with one point.

A huge advocate of preaching sermons with one point is Andy Stanley of North Point Community Church in Georgia. North Point is one of the largest churches in America. Stanley's sermons are heard by tens of thousands of people every week. Sure, Stanley is a gifted communicator, but he also knows his messages must be clear and easy to follow. If they weren't, he wouldn't have so many listeners. This is why virtually every one of his sermons has just one point.

There are other key benefits to designing a sermon around one point:

1. *You have time and room to develop your point.* Since listeners only have to keep track of one thing they can really absorb your message. There is nothing more frustrating than when a preacher touches on many key ideas or points but can't develop any of them because there are too many points and not enough time. Real opportunities for transformation are missed. I have heard more sermons like this than I care to remember. My colleague and friend Allen Johnson compares such sermons to someone leading you to the entrance of Disney World and telling you all about it but you are not allowed to go in. Now that's cruel!

2. *Your sermon will have drive and direction.* Listeners need to feel like a sermon is going somewhere in order to be compelled to pay attention. Remember that sermons must "begin, travel, and arrive." Preparing a sermon around

one point assures drive and direction because you have a singular target. A sermon with many points can feel like hitting every red light on the way to Disney World or, worse, getting lost on the way. Now that's frustrating!

3. *You only have one point to remember.* Having only one point makes your sermon much easier for you and your listeners to remember.

4. *You save time by putting aside other points for future sermons!* Were you planning on preaching a sermon with three points this Sunday? Wait a second! Why not use each of those points for a three week series? Bam! You now have three weeks of sermons planned. You're welcome.

You may feel tempted to jump to the next chapter and get on with the five steps but hold your horses! Before you can effectively apply this exciting method there is a crucial thing you must do: Come up with your point! Unless you have a compelling and clear point the method will not work for you. So first things first. Let's get to the point!

Getting to the Point

Imagine your scripture text is in front of you. If it actually is, great! You have chosen your text in one of two ways. Either a topic has led you to a text or the lectionary or a biblical theme has led you to a text. I know there is an ongoing debate about beginning with a text or topic. Later in this chapter I will address those two different approaches. At this point, just assume you have your text and you are ready to create your point.

Your next step is to exegete your text. I'm not going to spend time on biblical exegesis. There are plenty of excellent books and resources that can help you learn how to uncover a text's author, audience, context, language, form, and so on. In fact, you probably have these resources from your seminary or course of study classes. As you know, exegesis is a crucial part of the process of determining your point, so do your homework on the text.

Be sure to reflect on the text and wrestle with it on your own before you consult biblical commentaries. Commentaries can be helpful but commentators don't know you or your context of ministry. No one knows your congregation like you do. Most of all, God has called you, not the commentator, to proclaim the gospel to your particular congregation.

When you do finally consult commentaries find those that give more than "Bible trivia." Look for commentaries that have spiritual and theological depth in their interpretation. My experience has taught me that there are two types of commentaries: those for preaching and those for writing exegetical papers in seminary. I have found that some of the older commentaries are very "preacher friendly." A good place to start is to get a set of the original Interpreter's Bible commentaries (which are now out of print). They are pure gold. You may even find a retired minister who is willing to part with a set free of charge. If not, you can definitely find a set to purchase on the Internet. Many of the writers of these old commentaries were wise and gifted preachers who knew how to interpret a text for a sermon. You will find a treasure trove of sermon ideas in those dusty books.

Many of the newer commentaries are also very good. They contain the latest in biblical scholarship, which can be helpful. However, in their academic zeal some commentators forget that a large percentage of their readers are preachers seeking a message for a sermon.

Bottoms Up!

After you have done your homework on the text and have discovered its context and general meaning, you are now ready to discover your point. For many this is the most difficult part of the process of sermon preparation but it doesn't have to be. In fact, if you do it right it can be very rewarding not only for your sermon but also for your soul. Finding a point does take some time and investment but all you have to do is understand the text. Think I'm stating the obvious? Not really. To appreciate what it means to understand anything you need to hear from Janis Joplin.

Janis Joplin was a charismatic and pioneering singer in the 60s. Her stage presence and passion were penetrating. I watched a fascinating interview of her on YouTube. She was asked what made her singing so unique and powerful. She noted that unlike many singers she got "on the bottom side of the music."[5] She went on to say how many singers float on top of the music where the melody is. Her point of entry was the bottom side. That's what made her music and performances stand out. I thought that was one of the most profound things I had ever heard. Believe it or not, this idea is the key to finding the point of your sermon.

In order to find your point get on the bottom side of the text. In other words, *under*stand it. Have you ever really thought about the meaning of the word *understand*? It literally means to "stand under" something. When you stand under something you see the most vulnerable parts of it. Have you ever stood under your car with a mechanic? Have you ever heard someone say, "I am going to get to the bottom of this"? What about, "I love you from the bottom of my heart" or "I am going to expose the underbelly of the situation"? What all of this means is that you want to feel the vulnerability and heaviness of something, its very heart and soul. The bottom is where deep passions live. To use another musical example, listen to legendary blues artists. The blues is a genre of music defined by those who get to the bottom side of music and stay there. Ever watched footage of Stevie Ray Vaughan or B. B. King? If you can learn to preach with the same passion with which they performed their music you will have arrived as a preacher, my friend.

Get under your text and feel the soul, essence, and weight of it. This requires you to open your emotions to the text. One of the biggest mistakes preachers make when interpreting a text for a sermon is to make it only a cerebral exercise. They have nightmares of when they had to prepare an exegetical paper on Leviticus for their crusty Old Testament professor. Of course we must respect biblical scholarship and allow it to inform us, but we limit the text and our preaching when we don't allow our hearts to interpret scripture. Do you think the writers of scripture did not put their hearts into their writing? They were not robots. Ever read the Psalms? What about Lamentations? First Corinthians chapter 13? The Song of Solomon? Make sure the kids are asleep before you read that one!

In order to get to the soul of your chosen text you must open your heart as well as your mind. You do that by getting to the bottom side of the text and allowing it to reach the bottom of you. When you approach your text this way it will ensure you can express why the text is important to you. If you cannot express why your text is important to you, your sermon will never get off the ground. However, when you are able to share why your text is important your point will be compelling. When your point is compelling you will be inspired to preach with passion and conviction. Then your sermon will soar! Mark my words: Your point must be compelling and you must preach with passion and conviction in order to engage your listeners. If you are not passionate about your text and topic and compelled by your point, your listeners will not be either. If you have not been touched by the text how can you expect your listeners to be? Tom Long reminds us, "Eventually we will be the preacher of the sermon, but we must not forget that we will also be one of its hearers as well. When we go to the Scripture seeking not what 'the people ought to hear' but hungering ourselves for a gospel word, we will hear a word for them too."[6]

On a Beach and a Prayer

This sounds wonderful but how does this work exactly, right? Here's a prime example. I remember preparing a sermon series on the twenty-third psalm. Many folks in the church had requested a series on it, so I agreed. To be honest, I wasn't really that excited about the series. Like many familiar texts of scripture, I had repeated the psalm so many times that its meaning had diminished. In fact, it was quite depressing because I always repeated the psalm at funerals. I know the twenty-third psalm is very special to many folks, but when you lead funerals you read the twenty-third psalm a lot, and you are not very happy when you do it! I needed a fresh perspective badly, which is probably why I needed the sermon series the most.

I had to do something different to find a fresh approach to the twenty-third psalm. Reading it in my study next to the glare of my computer screen was not going to cut it. So I grabbed my Bible, smartphone, and headphones and drove my Jeep to the beach. I sat on the beach and read the psalm while listening to (are you ready for this?) "Kyrie Eleison" by the band Mr. Mister. It's a cheesy 80s pop song, but I love it. The message of the song was very appropriate for me. *Kyrie Eleison* is an ancient Greek prayer that means, "Lord, have mercy!" And that is exactly what I was asking the Lord for—mercy in helping me find inspiration for a sermon series! The Lord did have mercy on me. I found inspiration in the twenty-third psalm again and came up with two compelling points.

I found my inspiration by getting to the "bottom side" of the twenty-third psalm. As I was reading the psalm on the beach and listening to music, a big dark cloud started to form over me. It had been cloudy that day, but the weather forecast didn't call for any storms. However, I live in Florida where weather forecasts can be as reliable as a lottery ticket. It wasn't long before thunder started to roll, lightning began to flash, and the rain began to fall. So I ran back to my Jeep with my Bible and "Kyrie Eleison" still blaring in my ears. I was getting soaked, but somewhere between the beach and the parking lot inspiration hit me. The combination of the song, the storm, and fearing no evil "in the valley" sparked something in me, and it wasn't the lightning! In my own way I began to feel in that thunderstorm what it was like to walk through my own dark valleys. I connected emotionally with the psalm and suddenly a memory from my days in vacation Bible school came to me. I remembered a chant we shouted based on the twenty-third psalm: *Don't fear the valley!* I hadn't thought about that chant in years, but it is amazing how inspired ideas are teased out of you when you change your approach and open your heart.

As I sat in my Jeep with the rain pelting down on my soft top, I reflected on all the different ways God had walked with me through my valleys. I remembered how God had been faithful to me through pain, grief, temptations, mistakes, sins, feelings of hopelessness, and discouragement. I had never faced my valleys alone. God's grace and power always sustained me. The Lord had managed to shepherd me through my worst storms even when I was not a willing participant! It reminded me once again that verse 4 does not say, "in the darkest valley" but "*through* the darkest valley." The Lord will not allow us to stay in the valley. If we are willing to trust him, he will guide us through our valleys and use them for a great purpose.

After reflecting on these experiences, I remembered two ideas. The first was a quote by Frederick Buechner: "The resurrection means the worst thing isn't the last thing."[7] The second was that shepherds often lead their sheep through a valley in order to get to higher ground. The valley can be a great source of water and food for sheep. My experience on the beach combined with those ideas led me to create two compelling points. When I preached the sermon on verse 4: "Even when I walk through the darkest valley, / I fear no danger because you are with me. / Your rod and your staff— / they protect me" my point was *The worst thing is never the last thing.* When I preached on the last verse of the twenty-third psalm I ended the series with this point: *Sometimes the only way to the mountain top is through the valley.*

I drove home soaking wet that day at the beach, but I didn't care because I had found inspiration and had two compelling points that would preach! I changed my routine and opened my heart to the bottom side of the text, and it had reached the very bottom of me. I believe the Holy Spirit played a key role in finding my point. If the Holy Spirit inspires us during our sermon, we can count on the Holy Spirit inspiring us as we prepare it.

Name Calling

I recall another time I allowed the "bottom" of the text to reach the bottom of me. It wasn't as dramatic as my day at the beach but it was just as powerful. I was working on a sermon for the Sunday after Easter. They don't call it "Low Sunday" for nothing! In larger churches they should call it "Associate Pastor Sunday" because most senior pastors take that Sunday off, and for good reason! I always do, but at the time I was an associate pastor and had to pay my dues.

My text was John 20:11-18, when Mary Magdalene runs into the "gardener" at the tomb of Jesus. I had already come down from the high of Easter and was having a difficult time finding inspiration. I had tunnel vision on the text and was fixated on why Mary couldn't recognize Jesus. I read somewhere that her tears affected her vision. I thought that was a pretty lame explanation.

Then I looked at the very beginning of the chapter and read that Mary went to the tomb "while it was still dark" (John 20:1). Obviously, Mary couldn't see Jesus because it was too dark. So I went back to my text and verse 16 jumped out at me: "Jesus said to her, 'Mary.'" I wondered why the writer of John didn't just say, "And Jesus called Mary's name and she recognized Jesus." Then it dawned on me. The writer of John wanted to emphasize the sound of Jesus's voice speaking Mary's name. Mary recognized

Jesus by the sound of his voice saying her name. It was then I felt the bottom of the text getting to the bottom of me.

I imagined the sound of Jesus's voice calling my name. I tried to feel what that would be like. When I did, I was off to the races. All these ideas came flooding in to my head and heart. I remembered the time I was in a mall and saw a lost child run to the sound of his mother calling his name. I recalled when I was homesick the first semester of college and my dad calling and saying, "Charley, this is Dad." My dad's voice saying my name never sounded so good. The old saying came to me as well: "The sweetest sound people hear is the sound of their own names." I thought about the importance of remembering people's names. I went back to the text and realized that Jesus never forgets our names. The point of my sermon would be quite simply, *Jesus knows.*[8] Jesus calling out Mary's name signifies how intimately he knows and loves each of us. The love of Jesus is personal. Jesus knows. I could hardly wait to prepare my sermon! Low Sunday wasn't so low that year!

"Pour Some Scripture on Me!"

Allowing my heart to feel a text is the best way I know of to find inspiration. Silent prayer often helps open my heart to a text. I also find music helpful. I listen to hymns and Christian artists, but I also listen to secular music. I don't believe God is limited in the way God can speak to us. To be perfectly honest, I often prepare my sermons listening to hard rock and blues. It gets my juices flowing and helps me tap into my passions and convictions. Def Leppard and Stevie Ray Vaughan have often been helpful companions in my study!

Get out of your usual environment and routine and engage the text prayerfully and emotionally. Listen to music that inspires you. Reflect on your text beside the pool or lake. Take a drive with the top down. Draw pictures of your text or go for a walk in the park. Read your text to yourself at a ball game and see what happens. Talk to your buddies about your sermon on the golf course. Go see a movie with your text and sermon fresh on your mind. Put together a worship team and get new perspectives. Grab lunch with your colleagues and get their take on the text. Go to the airport and watch people. I've come up with a ton of compelling ideas and points while "people-watching" at the airport! Airports are filled with sermon material! I even did a sermon about what I learned at a bar and grill on the beach. That shook things up!

Sometimes I need more structure when seeking to find the bottom of a text. This is when I use a method called *lectio divina* (Latin for "divine reading"). It is an ancient prayerful approach to interpreting scripture. First, I *read* the text slowly. I then *reflect* on what I have read and jot down phrases or thoughts from the text that have touched me. Next I *respond* in prayer by expressing my thoughts and feelings to God. Finally, I *rest* in God and the text and seek to listen to God at the deepest level.[9] What I often find at the other side of this approach is either my point or the raw material for my point.

Lectio divina may not work for you. You may find another approach more helpful. The point is to do whatever will open your heart to the text and provoke passion in you. Allow yourself to feel the text and jot down whatever comes to you. You will be amazed at the memories, insights, ideas, and points that will come to you when you prayerfully engage the text with your heart. Be sure you are prepared to write down whatever comes to you. Sometimes, by the grace of God, the flood gates open and you want to capture as much as you can.

Are We Clear?

We have covered the importance of your point being *compelling*. This is your first and most important hurdle because if your point is not compelling it will not engage your listeners. Now we come to the second hurdle and that is making your point *clear*. Sometimes your point will be so compelling that it will be crystal clear. Other times you will have a general idea for a point that needs more focus. This is when you must do a little work on your idea to make it plain and accessible for your listeners. When you communicate your point you don't want your listeners struggling to understand its meaning. You will lose them. When you express your point, your listeners should recognize its meaning immediately.

I remember preparing a sermon on Romans 8:28-39. My focus was verse 28, "We know that God works all things together for good for the ones who love God, for those who are called according to his purpose." My general idea was that "God can take the bad circumstances of life and use them for good." It wasn't bad, and I could have prepared a sermon around that idea, but I wanted my point to have more focus and pop. I reflected on the text and read a few commentaries. I came across a wonderful thought. The word *crisis* in Chinese has two characters. One represents *danger* and the other *opportunity*.[10] So my point ended up being *God can turn opposition into opportunity*.[11] Now that'll preach!

Some preaching professors get really particular about creating a point. They will insist it be expressed in seven words or less and contain an active verb. Their textbooks often contain many pages explaining the importance of writing down a theme along with the text's focus and objective. You would think they were giving instructions on writing a dissertation. Those exacting guidelines might be helpful to some, but I have found them unnecessary. I have been preaching for over twenty years in local churches, and I've never felt the necessity for such rules. In fact, sometimes they can hinder my creative process. As long as your point is compelling and clear you are good to go. What has God laid on your heart to say? What did the bottom of the text say to the bottom of you? Express it in one clear and complete sentence.

Sometimes your creative juices will be flowing and your point will be terse and clever but that's not going to happen every time you prepare a sermon. So don't rack your brain trying to win a Pulitzer for every point. Just be compelling and clear. And don't think you have to be original. I hate to disappoint you but Mark Twain was right: "There is no such thing as a new idea." Sometimes the most powerful sermons help us understand familiar ideas in new ways. There is an added benefit to having one compelling and clear point for all of your sermons. At the end of each quarter and/or year you can publish a list of all your sermon points with their related scripture texts. Put them in the church newsletter and on the website. Post them on Facebook and Twitter. People will love it, and your sermon points will find a second life!

The Cart before the Horse?

You might be wondering if it is OK to have a point before you have a text. Of course it is! As long as it is compelling, clear, and you can find scripture to support it. Many faithful users of the lectionary think this is heresy. They insist you begin with a text before you come up with your topic or point. This is not practical or realistic. People often go to scripture seeking guidance on a particular issue. It is the issue or struggle that brings them to scripture. This is why topical preaching can be very effective. You begin with a topic people care about and then speak to the topic with scripture. If we believe the Bible is relevant why would we not embrace this natural approach?

I affirm the use of the lectionary and respect the discipline of beginning with a text, but whether we admit it or not, all of us bring our own baggage to every text. No one studies and interprets a text with a clean slate. This is why we must do our homework to be sure we are not forcing a text to say what it does not say. However, if we are open, the Holy Spirit will use what we bring to a text. Lectionary and topical preaching should not be at odds with each other. Both are valuable approaches to preaching. In fact, it is not necessary to choose one over the other. During particular seasons of the church year you may find lectionary texts very useful. At other times topical sermons might be the best option. Why not combine topical and textual approaches and preach on a biblical character or theme or do a series on a book of the Bible?

Where's the Handle?

Now we have come to the third and final hurdle in creating a point. You must express concretely what you want your listeners to do with your point. You have created a compelling idea you want them to know. Now you need to figure out what you want them to do. In other words, how will they apply the point to their lives? Every sermon needs a handle on it. Your point must be easily applicable. If your goal is to transform your listeners with the gospel they need more than knowledge—they need wisdom. And what is wisdom? It is the right application of knowledge. You must give your listeners direction on how to live out the message. The old preaching adage is true: Every sermon should answer two questions: "So what?" and "Now what?" Your point answers "So what?" Your application answers "Now what?"

Depending on the nature of your point your "handle" could be something as simple as leading your listeners in saying a prayer to profess or reaffirm their faith in Christ. It could also be out of the box like asking your listeners to leave their shoes at the altar for a homeless ministry. It could be asking each member of your congregation to commit to having a short time of devotion and prayer time each day. Why not challenge your congregation to invite one person to church the following Sunday or share their faith with a friend? What about asking your listeners to put their pledge cards on the altar? In one sermon I threw out beach balls into the congregation and they literally "had a ball" trying to keep the balls in the air. I told them their homework was to do something fun each day of the upcoming week and smile at one stranger every day. My message was that "joy" is one of the fruits of the Spirit! Again, how can your listeners apply your point? A sermon with no handle cannot be grabbed by your listeners and taken into their daily lives. It is left in the sanctuary. Literally tell them what to do.

When you have clearly answered "So what?" and "Now what?" congratulate yourself! The heavy lifting is over. You have a compelling and clear point you are excited about, and you have a concrete application for your point. Now it's time for some fun!

Turn to the next chapter and I will teach you five simple steps to your best sermon ever!

Remember

- For razor sharp focus prepare your sermon around one compelling and clear point.

- Find your point by getting to the "bottom side" of the text and allowing it to reach the bottom of you.

- Put a handle on your sermon by determining how your listeners will apply the point.

Chapter Three

The AGAPE Method

Five Simple Steps to Your Best Sermon Ever

Once you have a compelling and clear point and a concrete idea of what your listeners need to do you are ready to create an engaging and inspiring sermon. To get started I want you to think about roller coasters. Imagine being strapped in to a roller coaster and slowly clicking up the first steep hill. The butterflies in your stomach begin their flight patterns. You reach the top of the hill and the coaster slowly gains momentum and finally jets down with breathtaking speed. You take a sharp unexpected turn to the left. Then you go up and down again. You curve sharply to the right. Before you can catch your breath you turn upside down! The coaster then careens into the loading station, and it's time to get off. You can't believe the ride is already over! You feel exhilarated and satisfied. If the line is not too long, you may ride it again!

The truth is roller coasters wouldn't be as much fun if they just went around in circles or only went up and down. And it definitely would be a bummer if they didn't go very fast! Designers of coasters know that to create anticipation, excitement, and satisfaction they must be intentional about design.

In the same way you must take great care in the way you design your sermons. You don't want your sermons to only go in circles with no sense of anticipation or discernible point. You will make your listeners dizzy! You don't want your sermons to only go up and down with many ideas and points. You will wear your listeners out! And you certainly don't want your sermons to drag on as your listeners silently beg you to wrap it up! In order for your sermons to be engaging you must design them to start with a sense of anticipation, travel with the excitement of discovery, and arrive leaving a sense of satisfaction and inspiration. A wise teacher of preaching, Hal Luccock, said it so well many years ago: "The power of a sermon lies in its structure, not in its decoration."[1] It's not so much *what* your sermon says but *how* it says it that counts.

You are about to learn a foolproof method to designing engaging and inspiring sermons in five simple steps. This method, if followed correctly, guarantees your sermons will "begin, travel, and arrive"[2] in a way that will compel your listeners to put down their cell phones and listen to you. An added benefit is that this method will save you valuable time by getting rid of the guess work in choosing the appropriate sermon form. Should you preach like the great inductive artists and reveal your message at the end of your sermon? Should you preach deductively and break down your main idea? Or should you preach as an expositor by breaking down your scripture text? With this method you can do all three! These five simple steps combine all three preaching forms in a way that retain their strengths and discard their weaknesses.

This method is the perfect recipe for creating engaging sermons every single time.

Prepare yourself because you are about to craft your best sermon ever. You are going to learn what I call the AGAPE method. Each letter of the word represents a key step in the preparation of a sermon. More than that, the word *agape* reminds us that our goal in preaching sermons is to engage listeners with the gospel. *Agape*, as you know, is the Greek New Testament word for love that is selfless, sacrificial, and unconditional. It perfectly describes the redeeming love Christ demonstrated for us. The AGAPE method is a powerful preaching tool that helps us transform listeners with the love of Christ.

The AGAPE Method

Anticipation (create tension)
Grace (offer hope and guidance with scripture)
Answer (relieve tension with your point)
Proclamation (proclaim why and call to action)
Explosion (create an explosion of inspiration)

Step 1: Anticipation

Create Tension

So you are sitting at your desk staring at your point. How do you begin to prepare a sermon around it? How will you immediately capture the attention of your listeners? Simple. Think of your favorite movies, novels, and television dramas. What do they all have in common? Tension and conflict! All good stories create anticipation by establishing some kind of struggle and seeking to relieve it. This is what draws you into the story. If you have ever stayed up half the night to finish a mystery novel or "binge-watched" a series on Netflix you know what I am talking about. The anticipation of what was going to happen next had you hooked. The writers of these stories aren't dumb. They know exactly what hooks us—creating a problem and promising to solve it.

The easiest and quickest way to draw your listeners into your message is to create anticipation by introducing tension, mystery, or conflict and promising to relieve it, solve it, or resolve it. You must create anticipation rather quickly because listeners typically decide if a sermon is worth listening to in the first two minutes. I know that may seem daunting, but if you let anticipation do the work you have nothing to worry about. The truth is we don't like ambiguity. Our brains are wired to fill in gaps and hunt for answers. We are highly motivated to find relief from uncertainty. In step one you are allowing this urge to do the work for you. In his book *Communicating for a Change*, Andy Stanley notes that "People engage easily when they are convinced that you are about to answer a question they've been asking, solve a mystery they have been unable to solve, or resolve a tension they have been unable to resolve."[1]

For example, let's say you are preaching a message on prayer. You might begin your sermon by asking, "Do you ever struggle with prayer? Have your prayers ever gone unanswered? Do you wonder if prayer really makes a difference? Does it really work? And how does it work? I think if we are honest we have all asked those questions. Today we are going to discover how prayer really works." Or if your message is on solving conflict you may begin your sermon by talking about how difficult it can be to resolve conflicts with loved ones. You might describe a recent disagreement you had with a friend and say, "I imagine I am not the only one who has had disagreements with a loved one! What is the best way to resolve disagreements in a loving way? Well, I am glad you came to worship today because we are going to discover how to resolve conflict."

Ironically, **you begin your sermon preparation by going backward.** Think of questions, struggles, and experiences that will create a desire in your listeners to want to know your point. Think back on how you discerned your point from your scripture text. What questions or struggles did you have? What topic or tension brought you to the text? What led you to the "bottom" of your text? To borrow an idea from Eugene Lowry, see your point as the "scratch" to an unbearable "itch."[2] What will make your listeners itch?

An easy way to make your listeners "itch" for your point is to take a page out of the handbook of entertainment and use a "cliffhanger." Why do you think soap operas are still on the air? It is not because of the brilliant acting! It is because just about every scene ends with a cliffhanger. A scene will build to an inch of its resolution and then the director will cut to a commercial or to another scene. Your grandmother probably had better taste in television programs but she kept watching her "soaps" because she had to find out if Barbara was going to leave Johnny. A cliffhanger can be a very effective way to build tension in your sermon. Begin your sermon by naming the problem, mystery, or conflict and then illustrate it by telling a story without the resolution, promising to conclude it later in the message. This is what is known as a "tieback."

I used a cliffhanger when I preached a sermon entitled, "Why Am I a Christian?" I began the sermon with a story about speaking to a college sociology class. They were studying religion and wanted a local pastor's perspective. After some brief remarks there was time for Q and A. A young student raised her hand high. When I called on her she asked, "Why are you a Christian? I am taking a world religions class and there are so many beautiful religions in the world. I am wondering why you chose to be a Christian." I then asked the congregation how they would respond to that question: "If you were to have lunch with friends today and they asked you why you are a Christian, what would you say?" Tension was successfully established! If you are wondering what I told the student you will just have to wait until later in the book. See what I did there?

Once in a blue moon you will preach on topics that are so emotionally charged that you won't have to create tension. For example, on the Sunday after 9/11 no preacher in America had to create tension during the sermon. One Sunday my topic was *The Joy of Sex* and looked at sex as a healthy gift from God. I did not have to spend any time creating anticipation for that sermon!

Sometimes your scripture text will be intriguing and mysterious enough to create tension. Building a sermon around the inherent tension of a text can be very effective. For example, take the parable of the dishonest manager in Luke 16. The parable seems to encourage us to be dishonest and manipulative. Why would Jesus tell such a parable? And why would Luke place it immediately after the parable of the prodigal son? Or what about the story we read in the second chapter of 2 Kings when a gang of boys made fun of Elisha for being bald? Elisha responded by calling down a curse from the Lord. Two bears showed up and mauled forty-two of the boys. I dare you to preach your next sermon on that text!

It is helpful when your topic or text has enough tension to create anticipation for the listener, but it is not the norm. Most of the time you need to be very deliberate about creating anticipation in your sermon. If you struggle with creating an "itch," think like a journalist. My journalist friend Al Tompkins swears by five key motivators that engage people: money, family, safety, health, and community.[3] He bases these motivators on Abraham Maslow's hierarchy of needs. Wise journalists know these are primal drivers in people, and they gravitate toward stories that address them. As a preacher I have learned to add these motivators to the list: happiness, sex, power, purpose, self-confidence, recognition, curiosity, immortality, love and relationships, grief and suffering, morality, and stories that are popular in the media. See if your sermon topic or text relates to one or more of these motivators. If so, you are halfway home to creating tension. Simply ask yourself, "How does my point address and answer a question, struggle, or problem related to this key motivator(s)?" Express and describe that problem in step 1 and promise to solve it. Voila! Anticipation created!

I often find trending topics or hot news stories helpful in creating tension. They also freshen my message and engage listeners. For example, in November of 2015 there were two big news stories in one week. The week began with a controversy over Starbucks Christmas coffee cups. Starbucks decided to go with a plain red cup for Christmas instead of decorating it with snowflakes. In response, a fundamentalist Christian went on a video rant that went viral. He claimed that Starbucks's decision to remove snowflakes from their cups was a "crusade" against Christians and Christmas. It was a ridiculous notion because snowflakes are not even Christmas symbols. The news of this absurd video was quickly followed by reports of horrific terrorist attacks in Paris that killed over a hundred people. ISIS claimed responsibility. The whole world was reeling from that terrible event. The topic of my sermon the Sunday following those two news reports happened to be how to deal with stress! I had planned the sermon weeks in advance but at the last minute I inserted both of those stories in the middle of step one to help create the tension of stress. I talked about how both stories had one thing in common: the distortion of religion. I addressed the issue and honestly shared how the stories stressed me out. I told the congregation that I needed the message as much as they did, which is usually the case with my sermons! Those two big news stories were appropriately addressed and they helped to create tension in my sermon.

Sometimes you will preach on a text or topic that directly hits a key motivator. Preaching a stewardship sermon is a great example. Money is definitely a key motivator for people. I preached a stewardship sermon using the emotional need to hold on to money to create tension. I started my message by asking, "Why should you give your hard-earned money to the church? Has anyone ever given you a good answer to that question?" I went down the list of all the different nonprofit and charity organizations that ask for money and said, "We would go broke if we gave money to every worthy organization that needed it. Why should we give money to the church too? What makes the church more important than the Red Cross, Girl Scouts, or your alma matter?" I repeated some justifiable reasons people told me they didn't give to the church. I shared stories of people I knew who were hurt by the church. I kept hitting the question hard until they were almost begging for the answer. When it was time to turn to scripture (step 2) I read and expounded on 1 Corinthians 12:12-27, one body with many parts. I zeroed in on verse 27, "You are the body of Christ and parts of each other." I explained that the text plainly stated we as the church are the body of Christ. As the body of Christ we are God's chosen vessel in the world. How else is God going to get work done if not through the church? Then I gave them the answer (step 3): The reason we should give money to the church is because *the church is God's best hope for the world!* If I recall, that was a very successful stewardship campaign!

If you have ever taken a speech class you know that the beginning of your speech or your "hook" is the most important part of your speech. The same goes for your sermons. Step 1 is the most critical step of this method. If you do not create in your listeners a desire for relief from the tension, they will check out. Therefore, as you begin your sermon there are four critical things you must do:

1. *Make the tension personal.* Be sure to connect with your listeners by talking about your own struggle with the tension, mystery, or conflict you are addressing. What is your experience with the problem? Give examples from your own life. In order to engage listeners, they must relate to you and feel like you understand them. Without empathy your message has no credibility. Talk about your own struggles with prayer, faith, anger, difficult people, grief, temptation, discouragement, and so on. Don't use the pulpit as a confessional, but be willing to be honest and open. You must be real to your listeners. If you are not real, they will tune you out. Authenticity is crucial.

2. *Make the tension universal.* In order to get your listeners to want to spend the next twenty to thirty minutes listening to you, it is imperative that you make them feel the tension as well. How do your listeners experience the problem? You will have a variety of people listening to you so you must be intentional about reaching them. Describe and illustrate the tension in as many relevant ways as you can. For example, say your topic is "how to overcome temptation." Imagine all the different ways people face temptation, and be sure to name and illustrate them in your sermon. What tempts a middle-aged man on a business trip is not the same as what tempts an elderly couple filling out a tax return. Get my drift? Touch as many experiences of the tension as possible. Get as many people on board as you can before you move to the next stage of your sermon.

3. *Make a dead end.* To increase anticipation it is important to express how we try and fail at solving the problem,

39

mystery, or conflict. Not only is this a good rhetorical tactic, it also prepares our listeners for the transforming message of the gospel. Eugene Lowry calls it "the principle of reversal."[4] In order to prepare listeners for the impact of our message we must describe how we fall short finding answers to the problem. For example, is your sermon on the struggle to feel love and accepted? Think of all the futile and destructive ways people seek out love. When you name all the "dead ends," your listeners will be all the more ready to hear your answer or point on the love and grace of God. It will have maximum impact.

4. *Make a promise to deliver.* In order for your listeners to stay engaged they must know there will be a payoff to your message. Plainly tell your listeners the benefits of knowing and applying the answer. What difference will it make in their lives? How will it transform them? Why should they care about what you are going to tell them? Just as important, tell them the cost of not doing what you want them to do. What will happen if they ignore your message? Don't give away your point, of course, but drive home the advantage of applying the upcoming message and the disadvantage of not applying it. This increases anticipation. Will the message improve marriage? Strengthen faith? Offer salvation? Transform relationships? Prevent moral disaster? Build character? Ease anxiety? Provide reconciliation and healing? Motivate to serve? Inspire action that will change the world? What is the promise of your message? Why should your listeners keep listening to you?

I find it helpful to consider four different categories of listeners in this first step. I call them the 4 Cs. Just like diamonds are evaluated using 4 Cs (cut, clarity, color, carat), the sum of your listeners can be evaluated using 4 Cs: There are listeners who need to be *challenged* to grow in their faith. There are those who need to be *comforted* and encouraged. There are listeners who need to hear or be reminded they are *called* to serve in ministry. There are also skeptics and seekers who are *curious* about the Christian faith. You may have all four of these listeners in worship. Some may be in more than one category. Why should they listen to your sermon? Will your message speak to where they are in their journey of faith? Of course, every sermon is not going to reach all four categories, but it is useful to keep the 4 Cs in mind as you prepare your sermon.

Don't move to step 2 until your listeners are so fascinated they are virtually begging for the answer. You want to keep your listeners engaged and intrigued so they are dying to know what the Bible has to say about the issue you are addressing. Think of the tension you are creating like you are pulling a rubber band. The tighter you pull a rubber band the bigger the snap! You want to pull the rubber band as tight as you can before you move to step 2. If you create enough tension and are clear why the message is important, your listeners will be all ears. They will be eagerly awaiting the "snap" or the relief of tension. The bigger the tension, the bigger the snap.[5]

In a nutshell, **you want to accomplish two things in this first step: *"validate* and *fascinate."*** [6] Validate listeners by naming and describing their experience of the tension and fascinate them by promising relief of the tension and a valuable payoff. Communication expert Blair Warren reminds us that our need for validation is one of our strongest desires. What's more is that Warren believes that our desire to avoid boredom is just as strong. When we are fascinated by something it has our undivided attention.

Therefore, for Warren, validating and fascinating are the dynamic duo of persuasive communication.[7] William James was right: "What holds attention determines action."[8]

You will know you have effectively used the dynamic duo of validation and fascination when you hear this kind of feedback from listeners: "I felt like you were talking directly to me!" "Did you bug my house and listen to my conversations? How did you know I needed to hear a message on that?" "Have you been reading my e-mail? Maybe you can read my mind! Today's message hit me right between the eyes." Those are actual quotes from listeners after I have preached an AGAPE sermon. When your listeners feel validated in their struggles they will be fascinated to hear a solution. You will have their undivided attention. The power of anticipation will pull them through your sermon.

Step 1 is well suited for sermons on prophetic and controversial topics. There are times when we must speak truth to power and address a social or moral concern in our culture. These can be emotionally charged sermons that quickly turn listeners off. We have a much better chance getting more listeners on board when we begin by naming the tension of the issue from all sides and then leading our listeners to scripture to relieve that tension. Even if our listeners disagree with our position, they will appreciate that we began with their perspective and were willing to share our own struggle with the topic.

Step 1 also helps avoid the pitfall of the "curse of knowledge" that I mentioned in the first chapter. You are engaging your listeners by beginning with their experience and frame of reference. You are not assuming anything. You are asking the questions they are most likely asking. They are fully engaged and want to know more.

Chapter Five

Step 2: Grace

Offer Hope and Guidance with Scripture

You have created enough tension at the beginning of your sermon that your listeners are eager to find relief. You then turn to the Bible and, by God's grace, guide them to the answer. *Grace* is defined as God's unmerited favor and blessing. John Wesley also understood grace as God's influence and guidance in our lives. For Wesley, *grace* was not just a noun but a verb. God "graces" us. The nature of God is defined by what God does. Grace describes those loving acts of God that bring redemption and wholeness. The sermon is a vehicle for God's grace. Step 2 makes way for that grace as we open the scriptures. This means preaching can be a sacramental event. Surely we believe God is especially active during the sermon. I am mindful of John Wesley's pivotal experience of having his heart "strangely warmed" by the grace of God. It was not communion or baptism that penetrated his heart that special evening on Aldersgate street. It was the exposition of scripture. After all, Wesley did list "searching the scriptures" and preaching as "means of grace."[1]

You might be wondering why we didn't begin with scripture. There is a good reason for that. Many people in our culture today don't feel the Bible is relevant to their lives. They may see it as a nice piece of literature with wise lessons, but they certainly don't see the Bible as inspired by God. It's unfortunate, but it's the culture we live in. You cannot assume all of your listeners are waiting expectantly to hear scripture. You have to work harder than that. You must persuade them to want to read the Bible. And that is what you have just done in step 1. Your listeners are now eager to hear scripture. You've got them right where you want them!

During this step, consult all of your notes on your biblical text that helped you arrive at your point (chapter 2). Look over your notes carefully. What impressed you about the text? What did you find fascinating, intriguing, or interesting? Where was the tension in the text? Where did you feel the weight of the text? What did you feel at the "bottom" of the text? How did the text address your topic? What did you find challenging? What did you find funny or amusing? These are the things you want to bring out at this stage of your sermon. Remember, your purpose is to engage your listeners so you want to keep them engaged while explaining scripture. You do that by relating the text to your listeners.

When doing research for this book I posted a question on my Facebook page asking my friends what they looked for in a sermon. I was fascinated that the vast majority of responses included the word *relatable*. They appreciated when preachers made the lesson or text relatable to their lives. So when explaining the text be sure to relate it to the lives of your listeners. This is the time to be creative and have fun! Yes, preaching should be fun!

I once had a ball preaching on the wedding at Cana in John 2. The text has a gold mine of relatable material. I created tension by noting that Jesus's first miracle in John was not healing a blind man or raising the dead; it was turning at least 120 gallons of water into wine! Why? When the wine ran out, Jesus didn't say, "Well, I'll help you clean up. We have church tomorrow." No! He wanted the party to continue so he kept the wine flowing. No wonder the religious leaders accused Jesus of being a party animal! And the wine Jesus created was not the cheap kind you get in a box. It was the good stuff. The real expensive stuff! Jesus's mother was also at the wedding and she was nagging Jesus about making more wine. Even Jesus couldn't escape a nagging mother! Oh, and a wedding back in Jesus's day could last two weeks! Imagine the father-in-law getting that bill! I wonder if Jesus's wine was on the bill!

I drew my listeners into the text by connecting common experiences of weddings to the biblical passage. Don't worry. I did not tell my listeners that God is thrilled when we get intoxicated. The story is about the overwhelming generosity of Christ. The quantity of the wine symbolizes Jesus's extravagant love for us. God's grace and love are extravagant. This powerful message makes it clear why this miracle was first on John's list!

Think creatively and outside the box about your scripture text. How can you relate the Bible to your listeners? Don't just read the text and quickly move to step 3. Divide the text into verses, sections, or parts and explain and interpret it with curiosity, humor, and enthusiasm. Insert a relevant story or illustration to keep listeners engaged. Apply the text to today. Most of all, intersect the text with the tension you created in step 1. How does the text promise to relieve the tension? Don't get lost in the text and forget what drew your listeners into the text in the first place—the hope that their tension will be relieved.

I remember preaching on the faith of the Roman centurion in Matthew 8. The title of my message was "The Greatest

Compliment Jesus Ever Gave." Jesus saved his best compliment for a pagan soldier. Jesus told the centurion that he had never seen anyone with greater faith. The tension I created for the sermon was our struggle with doubt.

When I introduced the text I created more tension by lifting up the irony that our greatest example of faith in the gospels was not a disciple or even a Pharisee; it was a pagan man who was despised by the religious establishment. I pulled the rubber band even tighter by asking, "What the heck did this pagan do to impress Jesus so much? Why was his faith so unique? We are about to find out. And when we do we will be given the key to overcoming doubt in our lives." I walked through the text to find the answer. I focused on the centurion refusing Jesus's offer to come to his house to heal his servant. He felt unworthy for a visit from Jesus. This created more curiosity, so I begged the question, "If the centurion would not allow Jesus to come to his house, how was Jesus going to heal the servant?" The answer is found in the centurion's bold response to Jesus, "Just say the word and my servant will be healed" (Matt 8:8). The centurion was a high-ranking soldier, and when he gave an order it was done. He expected the same was true of Jesus. He had that kind of power, didn't he? I told my listeners that Jesus probably laughed joyously as he told the centurion he had just displayed the greatest faith he had ever seen. After the compliment Jesus said to the centurion, "'Go; it will be done for you just as you have believed.' And his servant was healed at that very moment" (Matt 8:13).

I explained to my listeners that the reason Jesus was so impressed with the centurion's faith was quite simple: he expected Jesus to act. The remedy to doubt is to doubt our doubts and expect Jesus to act. When we expect Jesus to act he will. Perhaps not in the way we expect, but Jesus will act. The point of my sermon (step 3) was *the more we expect Jesus to act the more reasons he will give us to believe.*

Notice that I added more tension to the sermon by lifting up curious aspects of the text. I also intersected the text with the tension of doubt by making the promise that the centurion's faith would give us the answer to overcoming our doubts. This was a fun text to preach because the conversation between Jesus and the centurion gave me different ways to relate the text to my listeners. The passage was also compelling because it was such a peculiar miracle story. This increased curiosity in my listeners and curiosity always pulls the rubber band a little tighter!

If you have a scripture text rich in content or large in size you can lift up observations of the text as "gateways" to your point. These "gateways" are not points but signposts to your point. They are observations of the text that arouse more curiosity as you build toward the snap of tension with your point. Therefore, they should relate to your point but never overshadow it. When used appropriately "gateways" can be an effective way to keep your listeners engaged as you guide them to your point.

I used "gateways" in a sermon on Jacob wrestling with God in Genesis 32. The tension I created in step 1 was, "How can we overcome our negative labels, especially the self-inflicted ones?" I lifted up Jacob as someone who was given a negative label when he was born. *Jacob* means "deceiver." As we know, Jacob lived up to his label. When I read the part of the story where Jacob wrestled with the angel I made this observation as a gateway: *when your identity is wrapped up in a label it can be tough to be pried away from it.* I expanded on that idea and related it to my listeners, but I kept things moving. Then I read God's question to Jacob in verse 27, "What's your name?" I made this observation about the question that served as a second gateway: *Jacob needed to admit who he was and what needed to change.* After I applied this idea to my listeners I then read the end of the story where God changed Jacob's name to Israel and proclaimed my point (step 3): *"God is more interested in your character than your comfort."*[2] Those two gateways kept my listeners interested and tracking as I led them to my point.[3]

In step 2 you must be intentional about keeping your listeners engaged. But have no fear. It's a cinch as long as you keep these two things in mind:

1. *Don't slow down!* Many preachers make the mistake of slowing down the pace of their sermons when they open up the Bible. Their speech gets slower, and they take on the air of a stuffy professor. All that momentum and anticipation is wasted and listeners are back to wondering if ice cream is on sale at the grocery store. You've lost them. So keep things moving! Stay passionate! Keep the same amount of energy you had at the start of your sermon. Move through the text long enough to explain and relate it and move on. Don't get bogged down in the text and focus on details that only you and your Bible professor would find fascinating. Remember your listeners can't wait for the answer, so keep moving!

2. *Don't overwhelm your listeners with scripture.* Sure you want your listeners to learn the Bible and be inspired by it, but "less is more" is a good rule of thumb here. Some preachers like to smother their congregation with scripture. I guess they think their sermons will be more "biblical" if they drown their listeners with the Bible. The Bible is inspired so it is a bit like shampoo or shaving cream. A

little bit goes a long way! Too much scripture can overwhelm listeners and cause "information overload." Of course, some texts are longer than others and you may need to use more scripture depending upon your topic and text. It can also be useful to draw on other scripture texts to support your sermon. Simply be mindful of the amount of biblical material you are giving your listeners. Use enough scripture to guide your listeners to your point and move to the next step.

Step 2 enables you to be an expositor of scripture, which is to deliberately break down, explain, and interpret your text. Exposition is somewhat of a forgotten practice in mainline preaching. This is unfortunate. Most listeners today have very little knowledge of the Bible. Now more than ever people need to be exposed to scripture. In fact, I have learned that people are hungry for it. Many listeners have told me that one of their favorite parts of the sermon is when I explain and interpret scripture. Your listeners will appreciate it too as long as you relate the text to their lives and keep things moving to the answer.

Chapter Six

Step 3: Answer

Relieve Tension with Your Point

Finally comes the moment your listeners have been waiting for. You have created anticipation through tension by presenting a problem, mystery, or conflict. You have opened up scripture to offer hope in relieving the tension. Your listeners are begging for the answer to the vexing question. They are eager for the big "snap" of tension. You have already done the heavy lifting of discerning your point from the scripture text. Now it is time to communicate it. Remember to connect your point to the question or struggle in step 1. You want them to experience relief from the tension.

As you were directed in chapter 2, be sure your point is compelling and clear so that listeners will remember it when they drive away from church. If some of your listeners are at Waffle House after worship and the waitress asks them what the sermon was about you want them to be able to rattle off the point. When some of your listeners are at a friend's house Sunday afternoon watching a football game you want them to be able repeat your point during a commercial.

You remember the cliffhanger I used for my sermon "Why Am I a Christian?" I am sure you have been dying to know what

I told the student who asked me why I was a Christian. I used the story for an advent sermon on John 1:14, "The Word became flesh / and made his home among us." My response to the student was also the point of my sermon: "I am a Christian because *religion is reaching for God; Christianity is God reaching for us.*"

I preached on Joseph from Matthew 1. I described the patience and courage he must have had to stick with Mary for nine months and actually believe she was pregnant with the son of God. I created tension by touching on the different ways we are tempted to lose patience and give up on our faith. My point was *patience is resisting the immediate to receive God's best.*[1]

I preached a sermon on Philippians 4:13, "I can do all [things] through him who gives me strength" (NIV). I described our struggle in finding strength for living. I mentioned that we typically fixate on the word *strength* in this verse when our focus should be on the word *do.* Paul found strength not by focusing on what he should have but by focusing on what Christ called him to do. Paul let go of the nonessentials of life and concentrated on the eternal. This is what gave him strength. My point was *let go of what you should have and grab hold of what you should do.*[2]

Your point can also be phrased in the form of a question. I preached an Easter sermon that asked the question, "If the same power that raised Christ from the dead lives in us then why don't we experience resurrection in our lives? Why don't we feel more empowered over the things that enslave us?" I focused on the stone being rolled away from Jesus's tomb. I wanted my listeners to release the things in their lives that were obstacles to experiencing resurrection. My point was *what stones need to be rolled away in your life?*[3] I named and described various stones that hold us back—bad habits, addictions, resentment, regret, guilt, and so on. I literally made the "stones" concrete!

It is important to make our ideas concrete for listeners. In step 3 don't just state your point, show it. Put skin on your message with an anecdote, metaphor, visual aid, or story. What does your point look like in real life? How does it sound, look, taste, feel, and smell? Engage the five senses. Be descriptive. How can you make the word become "flesh" for your listeners? Our school teachers knew what they were doing when they had us "show and tell." We preachers often skip the "show" and just "tell." Usually that is the "curse of knowledge" rearing its ugly head again. Don't just say it, show it.

I am going to practice what I preach and "show" you what I mean by making an idea concrete. Think of Velcro. The way Velcro works is quite simple. When seen under a microscope, the abrasive side of Velcro is made up of tiny flexible hooks and the soft side is made up of small soft loops. When you put them together the hooks latch on to the loops. That's what makes Velcro stick.

The mind understands and remembers an idea a lot like Velcro. Imagine the mind as a bunch of tiny flexible hooks. These hooks are eager to hook on to something to gain a better understanding of an idea. Now think of stories, images, and illustrations as small soft loops the mind hooks on to help bring clarity and concreteness to an idea. If an idea is connected to a powerful image, story, or metaphor it "sticks" to our minds like Velcro.[4] We think visually so our minds are always seeking to connect ideas with analogies and images. The lesson: if you want your listeners to understand and remember your sermons give them illustrations they can hook your ideas to. The image of Velcro just proved my point, didn't it? I bet you won't forget it!

A pastor once used a simple prop to make his sermon stick. During the sermon he invited a man to come up on the platform and stand next to him. The pastor handed the man a glass of water filled to the top and asked him to hold it for a moment. As the pastor continued to preach, he bumped the man's arm and water spilled on the pastor. The pastor turned to the man and asked, "Why did you spill water on me?"

The man replied, "Because you bumped me."

"I know I bumped you. But why did you spill water on me?"

"Uh—I spilled water on you because you bumped my arm."

"Let me put it this way: Why did you spill water on me? Why didn't you spill coffee? Or lemonade? Or tomato juice?"

"Because that's what was in the glass—just water."

The pastor turned to his listeners and said that every day we fill ourselves with good character choices or bad character choices. Inevitably, life is going to bump us around and provoke what is inside of us to spill out—fear, confidence, generosity, greed, humility, pride. What do you want to reveal?[5]

Now that message sticks, doesn't it? I know. You're probably already trying to find a way to fit it into your next sermon!

Let me give you another tool that will help you show your ideas. It is called "the ladder of abstraction." The ladder was introduced by linguist Samuel Hayakawa, and it is a communicator's best friend. At the top of the ladder are general and abstract ideas like faith, hope, and love. At the bottom of the ladder are concrete ideas like praying hands (faith), sunrise (hope), or the cross (love). Like a real ladder, the bottom of the ladder of abstraction is firmly supported by what is concrete—tangible words and descriptions. As you go up the ladder ideas get more general and abstract. Preachers are usually very good with abstract meanings, definitions, and concepts. What many preachers are not so good at is making ideas tangible and concrete. In order to engage and inspire listeners we must go all the way down the ladder and express our ideas concretely.

Consider the statistic that tobacco kills one in five Americans. It is a sobering statistic but probably not concrete enough to persuade a smoker to quit smoking. I saw a powerful public service ad that moved this statistic down the ladder of abstraction by humanizing it. The ad begins with a soldier who has come home from the battlefield to surprise his mother at work. He is hiding behind some boxes when she turns the corner and finds him. She erupts with a joyous scream and throws her arms around him. The screen goes black and these words appear: "Which moments are you willing to give away since every cigarette shortens your life. Tobacco is still killing 1 in 5 Americans."[6] Now that message "stuck" with me.

When you communicate the answer or your point, be sure to make it concrete for your listeners. This applies to the entire sermon as well. When you are preparing sermons always ask, "How can I make my ideas concrete, tangible, and applicable?"

You have finally relieved the tension for your listeners by communicating your point. Your answer is compelling, clear, concrete, and they feel the "snap" of tension. Now that your listeners have the point they need to know why it is important and how to apply it. You must proclaim your point and call your listeners to action. Enter step 4.

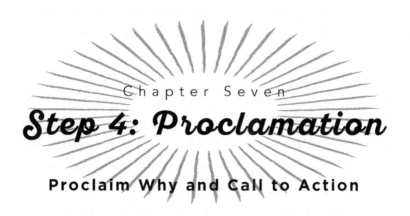

Step 4: Proclamation

Proclaim Why and Call to Action

Once you communicate your point and your listeners experience relief from the tension it is time to **move from explaining to proclaiming**. After all, preaching is more than teaching and explaining—preaching is proclamation! What is proclamation? It is a passionate declaration of a conviction or truth. For us that is the gospel of Jesus Christ! This is when you answer, "So what?" Why should your listeners care about your point? What difference does it really make? What do you think made Martin Luther King Jr.'s "I Have a Dream" speech so effective and memorable? King boldly and passionately proclaimed *why* his message of racial harmony was so important. Simon Sinek reminds us that King gave his "I Have a Dream" speech, not his "I Have a Plan" speech.[1] Listeners will not commit to your point until they know *why* it is important. Claim the authority God has given you, and boldly and passionately proclaim why your listeners should care about your message.

When I was a young pastor starting out I received a letter that transformed my preaching. The letter was from Bill Self, one of my preaching heroes. Bill was my pastor when I was a kid growing up in Atlanta. He was following my ministry and asked me to mail him recordings of my sermons. I reluctantly agreed, not sure what he might think of my preaching. A few weeks later I received his letter. He was quick to share that I was holding something back in my sermons. He sensed my reluctance to express my convictions. He stated that one of the reasons people come to worship is to be inspired by the convictions of the preacher. If preachers have been called by God to preach then their convictions that arise out of earnest prayer and preparation must be proclaimed. The truth must always be spoken in love, but if convictions aren't expressed preachers are not being faithful to their sacred task. So Bill told me to throw my head back and let my convictions fly!

I followed Bill's advice, and you know what I discovered? He was right! People resonated with my sermons like never before, and I began to see the difference it made in their lives and faith. A key aspect of engaging your listeners is being genuine with your convictions. When you stand before your people and speak from the "bottom" of your heart you will have their attention. The pulpit is the match that sets the church on fire. But the fire can't be started unless there is a strike of the match. Conviction is what strikes the match.

One of the essential elements of effective preaching that is lacking in the mainline pulpit today is bold and passionate proclamation. I believe there are three causes for this. One is the underlying idea that mainline Christians should be known for their reasoned and balanced faith and to preach with boldness and passion is somehow contrary to orthodoxy. Whoever said that good theology and bold proclamation are mutually exclusive? I know John Wesley didn't! Do you think thousands gathered around a tree stump to listen to him preach because he was dull? Wesley didn't lead a historic spiritual movement with dreary sermons.

The second cause of the lack of bold and passionate proclamation in the mainline church is the influence of the "new homiletic" on preachers. In the late 60s many believed preaching was dead. At that time everyone in authority was being questioned, and preachers were no exception. As a result, many seminaries all but neglected the importance of preaching and turned their attention to other areas of ministry. Thanks to Fred Craddock and his followers, a revival spread across pulpits in America that birthed creative ways of preaching that became less deductive and authoritative. This preaching revival became known as the "new homiletic." Much good has come out of the "new homiletic" and its inductive approach. The focus on changing traditional sermon structures to accommodate how listeners hear and process sermons has been a significant contribution to modern preaching. But the shadow side of the "new homiletic" is that it softened preaching and, more or less, turned the sermon experience into hearing a creative and artistic essay on scripture instead of a penetrating proclamation of the gospel.

The third cause of the lack of bold and passionate proclamation in the mainline church is the shift from rhetorical, oratorical, and "preachy" sermons to a more conversational style of preaching. This shift has been very important because conversational preaching certainly engages listeners a lot more than "top down" preaching. However, the downside of this shift is that many preachers don't feel comfortable preaching with conviction. African American churches seem to be the only churches not affected by this shift. Those of us not part of that tradition would do well to listen to sermons by African American preachers. We could learn a great deal about what it means to preach with conviction.

We must be sensitive to listeners and not turn them off by being "preachy." The good news is that the AGAPE method prevents that from happening. However, there is a time and place for bold and passionate proclamation. By the time you get to step 4, you have gained the trust and respect of your listeners, and they feel connected to you. They are open and eager to hear what you feel compelled to proclaim. I have discovered that listeners become even more engaged when you preach with passion and boldness. People are hungering for genuine expressions of truth, not preachers wearing skinny jeans sitting on stools trying desperately to appear trendy. Most of your listeners are also not looking to be impressed with your knowledge of the Bible and theology. They have not shown up for a lecture. They want you to speak from your heart to their hearts. When you get in touch with that you will find the sweet spot of preaching.

The absence of bold and passionate proclamation is one of the main culprits to the decline of the mainline church. This is the elephant in the room that is not being addressed. The pulpit is the engine that drives the train of the church. If the train is slowing down, the first place to look is the engine. You can have a balanced faith and preach with conviction, so throw your head back and let it fly! Your preaching will go to another level and people will respond to the gospel. Who knows? You may spark a revival in the mainline church!

If you are convicted about something and it flows from your point, go for it! Are you fired up about a social justice issue? Well, get after it! Does your heart break for the homeless in your community? Call your church to do something about it! Does your congregation need to be reminded that the church is not about them? What are you waiting for? Are you passionate about convincing those who have been hurt by religion that God loves them? Proclaim God's love like their life depends on it, because it does! Has it been awhile since your congregation has heard a message on the saving grace of God in Christ? It's time for you to proclaim!

At some point during your proclamation you must show your listeners how to apply your point. This is your "call to action." As I mentioned in chapter 2, every sermon needs a handle on it, something that provides a way to live out your message. This is when that idea takes center stage. So many sermons miss this key step. Most sermons answer *who, what, when, where,* and *why,* but very few answer *how?*

Love your listeners by helping them apply the message. This is the AGAPE method, after all. Is your message that we need to pray more? Tell your listeners to spend ten minutes in prayer every day for a week and experience the difference it makes to their faith. Is your message that nothing can separate us from the love of God? Tell your listeners to keep their eyes open for "God sightings" in their everyday lives and write those experiences in a journal. Is your message to get off your backside and serve Jesus? Tell them about the many opportunities for ministry in the church and have someone with a clipboard standing at the altar at the end of the service to sign people up. Try it. It works! And your faithful volunteers will love you for it! Is your message that Jesus Christ has forgiven sin and can make people whole? Give the invitation for listeners to receive Christ as Savior and ask them to come to the altar or pray at their seat. I know that one sounds obvious but it is amazing how many sermons present the gospel without offering an opportunity to respond. The gospel demands a response.

I have learned that it is effective to **repeat your point at least twice during step 4.** Your goal is for your listeners to remember your message. When you repeat your point it is reinforced in their minds. They will be able to take the point with them into their week. Repetition never goes out of style because it never fails to work!

At this stage of your sermon you have done something remarkable. You have combined three predominant sermon forms—inductive, expository (or textual), and deductive. You have created tension and relieved it with a scriptural answer (inductive). You arrived at your answer through an exposition of scripture (expository). Finally, in step 4 you have deduced why your point is important and how to apply it (deductive). You have used the strength of each sermon form to engage your listeners.

Before you move to the fifth and final step you will want to repeat the payoff. In step 1 you told them the payoff to keep them listening. Now you repeat the payoff to get them dreaming about how they will live differently as a result of your message. Tell them the difference applying the message will make in their lives. What will be the reward for living out the message? Get them excited and hopeful about what the message will do for them. This will lead nicely to the final step.

Step 5: Explosion

Create an Explosion of Inspiration

The purpose of the final step is to create an explosion of inspiration. You want your listeners to feel the power of your message and be motivated to live it out. See this step as the grand finale of a fireworks display, the big finish in a Broadway musical, Simba fighting Scar in *The Lion King*, Cinderella's glass slipper fitting her foot, or Ebenezer Scrooge doubling Bob Cratchit's pay. Need I mention the true "explosion" that changed the world? The resurrection of Jesus Christ!

It's time to bring out those moving, motivating, and inspiring stories and illustrations you have in your treasure chest of preaching goodness. Maybe the resolution to your cliffhanger in step 1 will be an effective "explosion." Perhaps it's time to use that profound personal experience of yours that you vowed would make it into a sermon one day. If it fits, go for it! Don't forget that the Bible is a great source for stories and illustrations! In fact, if your scripture text is a narrative you may not have to look any further than the conclusion of your text for the "explosion." You should use effective stories and illustrations throughout your sermon, but save the "big guns" for the final step.

I remember my "explosion" for the stewardship sermon I mentioned in step 1. I ended my message by telling an old legend about Zacchaeus, the short tax collector Jesus found in a tree. The legend goes that after his conversion it was Zacchaeus's habit to rise early and leave home for a while with a rake and shovel. Mrs. Zacchaeus noticed this one day and asked, "Where are you going?" Zacchaeus replied, "Do you remember that old sycamore tree I was in when Jesus found me? Well, I'm going to take care of it. It has been neglected by the city fathers and needs my care. You see, it held me so Jesus could find me."[1] I reminded my listeners that the church was the tree that held us so Jesus could find us. I told them it was now our turn to care for the church so Jesus could find others. Now that'll preach!

I recall preaching on the parable of the sheep and the goats in Matthew 25:31-46 and ending with a moving story. My focus was verse 40: "Then the king will reply to them, 'I assure you that when you have done it for one of the least of these brothers and sisters of mine, you have done it for me.'" I concluded the sermon by talking about the time I bought three hamburgers for a homeless man outside of a drug store. I had forgotten to buy another item at the store and when I returned five minutes later I saw the homeless man with an empty bag. He had devoured the burgers in minutes. He approached me with tears and said, "You are a true friend." I told my congregation that when he spoke those words I thought of the parable and felt as if it was Jesus speaking to me, "You are a true friend." I ended the sermon by repeating verse 40, "'I assure you that when you have done it for one of the least of these brothers and sisters of mine, you have done it for me.'" The following week I had several people in my church tell me they had engaged the homeless and bought them something to eat.

I concluded another sermon by talking about a conversation I heard between my chaplain supervisor in seminary and a patient. The patient was a well-known and respected man in the community who was recovering from a drug overdose. He was lamenting the shame of his condition to my supervisor. He expressed how his addiction had finally caught up with him and caused him to lose his reputation and respect in the community. He said, "I've lost everything. This is the end for me." My supervisor told him that he saw it as the beginning. The patient was indignant and asked, "What do you mean, the beginning?" The chaplain replied, "Well, if you have lost everything that means God has you all to himself. Just imagine what he can do with you now."[2]

Let's face it. Listeners will remember a good story or illustration long after they have forgotten our explanations and clever phrases. Remember, stories stick to the mind like Velcro. Why do you think Jesus told parables? Stories also penetrate the heart. Maya Angelou was right: "People will forget what you said. People will forget what you did. But people will never forget how you made them feel."[3] People are only motivated to do something when their heart is in it. Therefore, one of the best ways to motivate people is to create an emotional explosion with a good story.

Whenever you choose to tell a story in a sermon keep in mind that the most powerful stories are personal and have a shared context with your listeners. When you share a personal story, a deeper connection develops between you and your listeners. It also gives credibility to whatever topic or issue you are illustrating. If you get stuck and can't think of a good personal story, think again. Use these prompters: people, places, things, times, and events. Make a list of memories under these categories and a good story is bound to pop up. Communication expert Michael Port teaches speakers this trick, which is using the power of association to tease out stories.[4] Obviously, you don't want every story you share to be about you. You will turn listeners off. You also don't want to make yourself the hero of all your personal stories! Your listeners will start getting suspicious.

A word of warning about telling stories at any stage of your sermon: don't take too long telling a story. Long stories can be tedious for your listeners and kill the momentum of your sermon. Your purpose is to get your message across and for that message to stick. Telling stories is simply a tool to make that happen. We all know people who like to tell long, boring stories at dinner parties. Don't be that person in the pulpit (or anywhere else for that matter!). Tell stories that are worth telling and share them in a sensible amount of time. Unless it is an exceptional story or you are a world-class story teller, any story longer than three minutes is usually too long.

A powerful story can work well for step 5, but you don't always have to use a story. In fact, you shouldn't. You don't want to become too predictable to your listeners. You can also use a poem, poignant quote, testimony, video, or visual aid. Be creative and mix it up. Whatever you choose to do, "aim for the heart" and create an explosion of inspiration.

I once concluded a sermon using a powerful visual aid. I got the idea from Adam Hamilton. My sermon was on the parable of the rich fool and my focus was Jesus's statement, "One's life isn't determined by one's possessions" (Luke 12:15). I held up a small cardboard box and mentioned that just about every person living in a nursing home can fit everything they own in one small box. All they have left is what is most important to them—photos of loved ones, a Bible, letters and notes, pictures drawn by grandchildren. I then began to take out items in my box—a Bible, a cross, a picture of my wife, photos of family and friends, significant letters written to me. I told the congregation that these items are the most important to me because they point to the only two things that matter in life: our love for God and one another. Then I asked my listeners, "What will be in your box at the end of your life? What do you think will matter most to you? Why wait until the end of your life to focus on what really matters? Jesus said, 'One's life isn't determined by one's possessions.'"

Close the Curtain

Be sure to end your sermon soon after the explosion. Quickly tie in your conclusion with your point and "close the curtain." You want your listeners to leave worship moved and inspired. Let the explosion do its work and don't add to it. The quickest way to kill the power of the explosion is to prolong the sermon. Wrap it up and turn up the lights. Your listeners' hearts will be filled with inspiration and they will be ready to live out the message.

There you have it! The AGAPE method:

- Anticipation (create tension)

- Grace (offer hope and guidance with scripture)

- Answer (relieve tension with your point)

- Proclamation (proclaim why and call to action)

- Explosion (create an explosion of inspiration)

You now know the secret to great preaching and how to apply it. You are equipped to preach engaging and inspiring sermons that transform. The beauty of this method is that every step is designed to engage listeners. With this method you can't help but engage listeners. It is virtually guaranteed. Now turn to the next chapter and let's put it all together.

Remember

- Step 1: Begin your sermon by immediately creating anticipation by introducing tension, mystery, or conflict and promising to relieve it, solve it, or resolve it.

- Step 2: Offer God's hope and grace with scripture by relating the text to the tension.

- Step 3: Relieve the tension by communicating and showing the answer (point).

- Step 4: Proclaim why your point is important and call listeners to action (repeat your point at least twice in step 4 and end step 4 by repeating your payoff).

- Step 5: Create an explosion of inspiration in the hearts of your listeners with an illustration, story, video, or visual aid (conclude your sermon soon after the explosion of inspiration).

Putting It All Together

We have focused on each step of the AGAPE method. Now let's put all of the steps together and learn why this method is so irresistibly effective. As we do, I will give you some important final instructions so you can be on your way to preparing your best sermon ever. Let's begin by taking a look at three outlines of sermons I referenced in the book. As you read, notice the flow or pattern of the method.

"The Greatest Compliment Jesus Ever Gave"

Anticipation: How do we overcome our doubts?

Grace: Matthew 8:8-15—Jesus compliments the Roman centurion on his great faith. He expected Jesus to act in his life.

Answer: The more we expect Jesus to act the more reasons he will give us to believe.

Proclamation: The remedy to doubt is to doubt our doubts and expect Jesus to act. When was the last time you expected Jesus to act in your life? *Call to action*: Receive encouragement by remembering a time when Jesus acted in your life. Pick an area of need in your life and pray, expecting Jesus to act.

Explosion: The story of meeting my wife has taught me to believe in Jesus's faithfulness and guidance!

"Why Give Money to the Church?"

Anticipation: Why should you give your hard-earned money to the church?

Grace: 1 Corinthians 12:12-27—one body with many parts. Verse 27: "You are the body of Christ and parts of each other."

Answer: The church is God's best hope for the world.

Proclamation: History reflects that when God does something significant in this world it is accomplished through the church. As the body of Christ we are God's chosen vessel in the world. How else is God going to get work done if not through the church? *Call to action*: Place your pledge cards on the altar.

Explosion: Legend of Zaccheus taking care of the sycamore tree he climbed to see Jesus. He reminds his wife that it was the tree that held him so Jesus could find him. The church is the tree that holds people so Jesus can find them.

"The Secret"

Anticipation: How do we find strength for living? How do we find the power to keep going when we want to give up?

Grace: Philippians 4:10-13—"I have learned the secret of being content in any and every situation. . . . I can *do* all [things] through him who gives me strength" (NIV, emphasis added). Paul's secret to strength and contentment lay in learning to focus on what he was supposed to do, not what he felt he should have.

Answer: Let go of what you should have and grab hold of what you should do.[1]

Proclamation: You want power? Take your mind and heart off the nonessentials and focus on the eternal. Christ loves giving strength to those who want to be involved with what he is doing in the world. *Call to action*: Give a cup of cold water in Jesus's name. Make yourself available to God and watch your life transform. You will be so alive you will forget about getting everything you want. You will find the secret to contentment.

Explosion: Scene from the movie *The Shawshank Redemption*: "Get busy living or get busy dying."[2] Get busy living for Christ or get busy dying in trivial pursuits.

The Magic Formula

A significant reason why the AGAPE method is so effective is because it follows the same pattern or formula of many of your favorite books, movies, and television shows. For example, every Disney movie follows virtually the same pattern as the AGAPE method. They just don't call it by that name. Let's take the insanely popular movie *Frozen*:

- Elsa injures her sister Anna (**conflict—tension**).

- Olaf teaches Anna about sacrificial love (**lesson—answer**).

- Anna sacrifices herself for Elsa (**call to action**).

- Anna is revived, and Elsa is redeemed. Elsa's love controls her powers for good, and she makes snow for the kingdom (**explosion of inspiration**). You probably noticed that Anna is the "Christ figure" in the movie.

Chapter Nine

If *Frozen* is not your thing, what about *The Lion King*?

- Mufasa is killed and Simba, Mufasa's son, believes he is responsible (**conflict—tension**).

- Simba runs away but then is told by Mufasa in a vision to "remember who you are" (**lesson—answer**).

- Simba returns home (**call to action**).

- Simba defeats Scar, takes back the land, and paradise is restored (**explosion of inspiration**).

This pattern is not only in Disney movies. What about the Christmas classic *A Charlie Brown Christmas*?

- Charlie Brown is sad and struggles with the meaning of Christmas (**conflict—tension**).

- Linus tells Charlie Brown what Christmas is all about by quoting Luke 2:9-12 (**lesson—answer**).

- Charlie Brown takes the needy Christmas tree (representing Christ) home with him to decorate it (**call to action**).

- Charlie Brown's friends follow him home and help him decorate the tree. They all wish him "Merry Christmas" and sing "Hark the Herald Angels Sing" (**explosion of inspiration**). There is a reason why that animated Christmas special has been on television every holiday season for over fifty years!

Consider the parable of the good Samaritan (Luke 10:25-37). Jesus affirms the importance of loving our neighbor. A religious man asks Jesus, "Who is my neighbor?" Jesus responds by telling a story:

- A man is attacked by robbers and left half-dead. "Religious" people walk by and ignore him (**conflict— tension**).

- The "outsider" or enemy (Samaritan) has compassion on the beaten man (**lesson—answer**).

- The Samaritan heals his wounds and carries him on his donkey to an inn and pays for the man to be looked after (**call to action**).

- After telling the story Jesus asks the religious man who was truly "a neighbor" to the injured man, and he replies, "The one who demonstrated mercy toward him" (notice he could not say "Samaritan"). Jesus responds, "Go and do likewise" (**explosion of inspiration**).

As you can see from some of the stories described, quite often the conflict or tension is about *unfairness* or the *separation from a loved one.*[3] These two types of conflict are powerful and resonate deeply with people. Keep that in mind as you choose topics, illustrations, and stories for your sermons.

Tricks of the Trade

When you compare the AGAPE method to the powerful narratives just mentioned you see that it hits three essential targets within listeners: the heart, mind, and will. They feel a problem, learn a lesson or solution, and are motivated to act on it. Engaging sermons enable listeners to feel, know, and do, and in that order.

Listeners must be moved emotionally before they are persuaded to learn. They must learn in order to know what to do. Then they must be inspired to do it. If your goal in preaching is to transform listeners with the gospel then your sermon must accomplish all three.[4]

The aforementioned examples also demonstrate that the AGAPE method creates a sermon structure that is agreeable to listeners. Our brains are the most alert at beginnings and endings. When preachers begin a sermon we are all ears. Likewise, when they say "In conclusion" we are especially attentive![5] One of the secret ingredients of the AGAPE method is the three satisfying movements that have both a distinct beginning and ending. The first movement begins with anticipation and ends with an answer. The second movement begins with the proclamation of the answer and ends with its application. The third movement is the explosion itself, which often begins with a story or illustration and ends with the climax and conclusion. There are three beginnings and three endings in this sermon structure. This means your listeners will be at the height of their alertness six times during your sermon. This dramatically increases your listeners' ability to track your sermon and absorb your message.

One of the "tricks of the trade" of every effective communicator is being mindful of the attention span of listeners. Dr. Harrison B. Summers taught radio and television broadcasting at Ohio State University. He did extensive research on what holds the attention of listeners and viewers during broadcast programs. Summers's expertise and years of experience produced the secret to holding people's attention: **"Give the listener something new at frequent intervals."**[6] The AGAPE method is designed to do just that. The five steps produce a fascinating trip with enough twists and turns to keep listeners interested and engaged.

I encourage you to keep Summers's conclusion in mind as you prepare the content of each step. Have you ever sensed listeners connecting with you through an entire sermon but could not figure out what you were doing differently? Chances are it was because you presented something new at frequent intervals without knowing it. I am always intentional about expressing my ideas in different ways throughout my sermon to keep listeners engaged. There are several ways to do this: tell a story, use an illustration or metaphor, ask rhetorical questions, or relate your text to current events. You can also show a picture or video, use a visual aid, present a skit, or have someone share a testimony.

A powerful way to introduce something new to listeners is to contrast ideas and emotions. Communication expert Nancy Duarte believes that if you want to keep listeners engaged "contrast is key."[7] Next time you watch your favorite television show notice how often moods or emotions shift within each scene. This is intentional. Creators of television shows know that to keep listeners engaged they must contrast emotions frequently. Apply this tactic in your sermons by moving your ideas, illustrations, and stories from the head to heart, abstract to concrete, sad to happy, fear to peace, doubt to faith, struggle to grace, devastation to celebration, or as Duarte likes to put it, "from *what is* to *what could be*."[8] As you might have guessed, the power of contrast is inherent to the AGAPE method—problem to solution, application to explosion.

The lesson is to do anything that will bring variety to your movement of thought. Variety in presentation is the spice of good sermons.

Variety is also important in sermon delivery. When natural and appropriate vary your volume, pace, and pitch. Don't have a dreaded monotone delivery. Be especially mindful of your rate of speech and use of pause. Those two elements of delivery are often overlooked, but they are vitally important. In my years of preaching I have learned that people think faster than they hear, so if you speak too slowly their minds will wander. Yes, some preachers speak much too quickly and need to slow down. However, in my experience many preachers speak too slowly. You want to speak fast enough so that the quick minds of your listeners are comfortable tracking your sermon. Speaking at a comfortably swift pace conveys enthusiasm and urgency. It also makes slowing down and pausing that much more effective. You need pauses throughout your sermons for dramatic effect and to give listeners time to reflect.

Learning to deliver a sermon effectively takes some practice, but it is easier than you think. Listen to recordings of your sermons and imagine yourself as one of your listeners. Also be sure to watch your sermons and evaluate your appearance and body language. Many preachers don't like to watch themselves preach, but you can't grow as a preacher unless you do. It is also very helpful to observe news anchors, comedians, motivational speakers, and TED Talk presenters to study how they keep listeners engaged.

Always consider the listener's perspective during your sermon. Imagine each of the five steps as its own little trip. How are your listeners experiencing your content and delivery? Is the trip a slow silent ride down a flat road surrounded with nothing but cow pasture or is the trip filled with peaks and valleys, fun twists and turns, and beautiful sights and sounds?

Put Some Meat on Those Bones

It is important to see the flexibility of this sermon design. Don't look at this method rigidly, like there is no room for your own contribution. See this framework like a skeleton. Add whatever meat to the skeleton you desire. How you put the sermon together is up to you. Just be sure to follow each step. The flow of your sermon may look something like this:

tension → "cliff hanger" illustration → video → **scripture** → illustration → **point** → visual aid → **proclamation and call to action** → **"cliffhanger" resolution (explosion)**

Or it may look something like this:

tension → **scripture** → personal story → **point** → statistics → illustration → **proclamation** → **call to action** → **visual aid (explosion)**

Or it may look like this:

tension → **scripture** → lay testimony → **point** → humorous anecdote → **proclamation** → personal testimony → **call to action** → **illustration (explosion)**

Or it could be as simple as this:

tension → personal story → humorous anecdote → **scripture** → **point** → **proclamation** → story with an image on screen → **call to action** → **video (explosion)**

Again, these are just examples. There are a variety of ways you can put together an AGAPE sermon.

Be sure to make effective transitions as you move from one step to the next. A good rule of thumb is to **make at least two transitional statements between steps**. This will mentally prepare your listeners that you are shifting to another movement of thought. If you don't give your listeners an indication of where you are going they may lose track of your sermon. For example, if your sermon is on prayer and you are moving from tension to scripture (step 1 to step 2), you might say, "We are not the only ones who have struggled with prayer. Believe it or not the disciples had questions about prayer too. They noticed Jesus habitually praying and wondered how it worked. Let's take a look at what Jesus had to say to his disciples about prayer. I believe we will find some answers to our questions." Your listeners are now eager to hear what Jesus had to say about prayer.

It's about Time

The AGAPE method is helpful in its flexibility with sermon length. Length of sermons vary, depending upon your tradition. Some preach ten- to fifteen-minute homilies. Others preach for thirty minutes. Still, some preach forty-five minutes to an hour. The AGAPE method is one size fits all. Because you only have one point and five steps you can tailor this method to any sermon length.

Regardless of how long you preach **be mindful of the length of each step.** You don't want to spend so much time on one step that you shortchange the others. The time you spend on each step will vary depending upon your text and topic. Just remember that each step plays a critical role in the creation of an engaging and inspiring sermon. The longer you use the AGAPE method the more you will develop time instincts for each step.

Outline or Script?

I am frequently asked, "Do you prepare an outline or a manuscript?" I have experimented with both and have found a script works best for me. A script may not work for you. You may feel more comfortable preparing an outline or notes of your thoughts. The key is to find what fits you and communicates best to your listeners. Tom Long said that effective preaching is about balancing "precision of language and connection with listeners."[9] Both are essential to an engaging sermon. For me to have precise language I have to "talk out" a script. This is known as preparing an "oral manuscript."[10] I actually preach my sermon into existence. I also visualize preaching to my congregation as I prepare my script. I have found that preparing orally increases creativity and sharpens verbal skills. It also triples the speed of ideas. A mistake many preachers make is putting sermon preparation into two categories—getting the sermon manuscript or outline written and then getting ready to deliver it. I have discovered that the most effective and efficient way for me to prepare sermons is to have delivery in mind from the beginning by preparing an oral manuscript.

When I prepared a sermon outline I repeated myself, stumbled over transitions and illustrations, and didn't have any sense of timing or momentum. I have learned through trial and error that I must "clear a path" with a script. This way I am confident about my language and know where I am going. I do stray from the path when led, but I always know where the path is and how to get back on it. Preparing a script also gives my sermons a second life. Every week I publish an edited sermon manuscript. These are distributed for free throughout the church and community.

When I first realized that preparing a script worked best for me I knew it was only half of the preaching equation. It didn't matter how good my content was if I could not look my listeners in the eyes and connect with them. I wasn't going to read my script. People can read a sermon at home! So there was only one option: memorize my script. But I do more than just memorize my sermon. I don't want to sound like a robot repeating verbatim what is on the page. I want the delivery of my words to be fresh and conversational so I also internalize as I memorize. I make certain my sermon will come from the very "bottom" of me. To do this I always rehearse my sermon several times. Because I prepare an oral manuscript, rehearsing the sermon feels natural. It also helps me to discard, change, or rearrange what sounds awkward or out of place. When it is time to preach I don't just know my message, I embody it. It is a part of me. I know my "path" so well that I can preach from my heart and not feel tied to a script. I feel free to expand or adjust parts of my sermon in the preaching moment when needed. The more I rehearse my sermon the more freedom I have in the pulpit.

Whether you prepare an outline or script, the practice of rigorously rehearsing sermons is what separates good preachers from great preachers. If the idea of rehearsing sermons doesn't sit right with you, consider this: What if your praise band and/or choir never rehearsed before worship? What would you do? You would get another director!

So here are my three steps to dynamic delivery: memorize, internalize, and rehearse. It works for me. Whatever you do to prepare your sermons be sure it equips you to preach from your heart and engage your listeners.

Remember

- To hold attention give your listeners "something new at frequent intervals."[11]

- Make at least two transitional statements between steps.

- Prevent shortchanging a step by being mindful of the time you spend on each step.

- Prepare a sermon that balances "precision of language and connection with listeners."[12]

- Try memorizing, internalizing, and rehearsing when preparing to deliver your sermon.

Conclusion

The AGAPE method gets results. Since I started using it on a regular basis I have been amazed at the outcome. Listeners have a deeper connection with me as I preach. More people sign up to serve in ministries. More people are studying the Bible on their own and growing in their faith. There is an increase in requests for copies of my sermons and more hits on our sermon videos. People use my sermons for home Bible studies, and they are excited about inviting their friends and neighbors to worship. Those who attend sermon talk-back groups are engaged and eager to share feedback and ask questions. What I find most rewarding are the positive responses I receive from skeptics and seekers. It is clear that this method of preaching appeals to those who are curious about the Christian faith. More and more "curious" listeners are attending worship and asking me questions about my sermons. Many of these conversations have led them to follow Christ. Isn't that what it's all about? What's more is that people who have not been inside of a church in years because of past "church trauma" are connecting with the church and reaffirming their faith in Christ. I can trace all of these results back to when I made the decision to use the AGAPE method.

By the grace of God, the AGAPE method works! The reason is simple. When you engage listeners by validating their struggles and problems, fascinate them by guiding them to a biblical answer, speak from your heart to their hearts, and move them to action, lives are transformed for Christ.

I have also experienced great joy seeing ministers improve their preaching by using the AGAPE method. When I teach the AGAPE method in classes, seminars, and workshops I see preachers transform before me. I recall a woman in one of my classes who was unsure of being called to preach. When the class concluded, her call was confirmed and she felt empowered as a preacher. Another minister told me that the AGAPE method has invigorated his ministry. Congregants keep asking him, "What has gotten into you? You are on fire!" Another local pastor told me that the AGAPE method saves him valuable hours in sermon preparation. He used to spend hours spinning his wheels trying to figure out how to put his sermons together. Now he begins sermon preparation with confidence and enjoys preaching again.

I am not claiming the AGAPE method is a silver bullet for preaching, but it comes pretty darn close. Results will vary, but one thing is sure: if you commit to using it you will see results in your ministry.

The AGAPE method is not the only way to prepare effective sermons. There are other valuable sermon forms you should use to vary your approach.[1] You don't want to become too predictable to your listeners. Nevertheless, the AGAPE method is a simple repeatable process for creating engaging and inspiring sermons time after time. It is my "go-to pitch" that gets results. It will for you too.

For your convenience I have provided a quick reference guide for sermon preparation. If you can answer each of the guiding questions you will have the ingredients for an engaging and inspiring sermon.

To see examples of the AGAPE method go to my website www.charleyreeb.com. There you will find AGAPE sermon scripts and videos to help reinforce your learning of this method. You will also find several helpful videos and blogs on preaching.

I would love to hear from you! Let me know how I can help you. You can contact me at charley@charleyreeb.com.

Now get after it! You have all you need to prepare and deliver sermons "that'll preach!"

Quick AGAPE Guide for Sermon Preparation

And Your Point Is?

- How does your scripture text speak to the "bottom" of you?

- What is the point of your sermon? (In one clear and compelling sentence.)

- Are you passionate/excited about your message? (If not, find something else to preach about!)

- *Why* are you passionate about your message?

- How can your listeners apply your message? (What is the call to action?)

- What stories, illustrations, anecdotes, and so on come to mind?

Anticipation

- What problem, mystery, or conflict creates a strong desire to know your point?

- How do you experience the problem?

- How do your listeners experience the problem?

- How do we fail at solving the problem?

- How will your listeners benefit from knowing the answer?

- What are the costs of ignoring the answer?

Grace

- How does the scripture text address the tension and give hope to the problem?

- What do you find fascinating, funny, or exciting about the text?

- How does the text touch the "bottom" of you?

- How does the text relate to the lives of your listeners?

Answer

- What is the answer (point) to the problem?

- How does your point solve the problem?

- How can you "show" your point and make it concrete?

Proclamation

- Why should your listeners care that your point solves the problem?

- What convictions arise when you reflect on why the point matters?

- How do listeners apply the point? (What is their *call to action*?)

- What is the reward for applying the message?

Explosion

- What ideas, illustrations, or stories will inspire your listeners to live out your message?

Acknowledgments

Publishing a book is a team effort. I have had the privilege of working with a stellar team at Abingdon Press. I want to thank Paul Franklyn for his encouragement. I want to thank Connie Stella for believing in this book and offering invaluable wisdom and guidance. I also want to thank my production editor, Laura Wheeler. Her careful and skilled attention to this project from beginning to end was essential to the birth of this book. Stephen Graham-Ching was a pleasure to work with and provided helpful support. I also must thank Peggy Shearon for her indispensable work behind the scenes and Jeff Moore for creating the cover of this book.

I want to express my appreciation for those who have helped to shape my preaching. There are four works that have had a significant influence on me as a preacher: *In the Minister's Workshop* by Halford E. Luccock, *The Homiletical Plot* by Eugene Lowry, *Surviving the Stained-Glass Jungle* by William L. Self, and *Communicating for a Change* by Andy Stanley. I'm also grateful for the mentors and heroes of mine who have made a profound impact on my preaching ministry: Brad Dinsmore, Bill Self, Ed Beck, Riley Short, and Allen Johnson. I am indebted to Al Tompkins of the Poynter Institute for his insights on communication theory. Many of our conversations served as fodder for this book.

I also want to thank my students in the course of study program at Candler School of Theology and License to Preach School at Florida Southern for their support. Their feedback helped hone the material in this book.

I must thank Pasadena Community Church (UMC) whom I have the privilege to serve. They were the laboratory for testing the ideas in this book. I am grateful for their love, faithfulness, and support. It is an honor to be in ministry with them.

Most of all, I am eternally grateful to my wife, Brandy, for her endless love and support. She listened patiently and offered wise guidance throughout the writing of the manuscript.

Notes

1. The Problem and the Solution

1. J. Wallace Hamilton, "Sermon Preparation" (essay, Pasadena Community Church, St. Petersburg, FL, n.d.).

2. Chip and Dan Heath, *Made to Stick: Why Some Ideas Survive and Others Die* (New York: Random House, Inc., 2007), ebook edition, introduction.

3. John Wesley, "Sermons on Several Occasions: Preface, 1746," *Sermons 1*, The Bicentennial Edition of the Works of John Wesley, ed. Albert C. Outler (Nashville: Abingdon Press, 1984), 1:104.

4. Ibid.

5. Hamilton, "Sermon Preparation."

6. Heath and Heath, *Made to Stick: Why Some Ideas Survive and Others Die,* ebook edition, introduction.

2. And Your Point Is?

1. *Planes, Trains and Automobiles*, DVD, directed by John Hughes (1987; Hollywood, CA: Paramount Pictures, 2000).

2. Ken Untener, *Preaching Better: Practical Suggestions for Homilists* (New York: Paulist Press, 1999), ebook edition, chap. 8.

3. Attributed to Howard Hendricks.

4. Quoted in David L. Larsen, *Telling the Old, Old Story: The Art of Narrative Preaching* (Grand Rapids, Michigan: Kregel Publications, 1995), 67.

5. "Janis Joplin [on] European audiences," YouTube video, 7:41, from The Dick Cavett Show on July 18, 1969, posted by "cavettbiter," October 26, 2008, https://www.youtube.com/watch?v=CmgSzbdL1So.

6. Thomas G. Long, *The Witness of Preaching*, 2nd ed. (Louisville: Westminster John Knox, 2005), ebook edition, chap. 2.

7. Frederick Buechner quotes, AZ Quotes, accessed November 7, 2016, http://www.azquotes.com/quote/859029.

8. Point inspired by the hymn "Jesus Knows" by Daniel O. Teasley (1907).

9. I base my approach to *lectio divina* on the instructions from the following website: http://ocarm.org/en/content/lectio/what-lectio-divina.

10. John F. Kennedy, "Remarks at the Convocation of the United Negro College Fund" (speech, April 12, 1959, Indianapolis, IN), https://www.jfklibrary.org/Research/Research-Aids/JFK-Speeches/Indianapolis-IN_19590412.aspx.

11. Charles D. Reeb, *One Heaven of a Party* (Lima, OH: CSS Publishing Company, 2003), 133.

3. The AGAPE Method

1. Halford E. Luccock, *In The Minister's Workshop* (New York: Abingdon-Cokesbury Press, 1944), 118.

2. Quoted in Larsen, *Telling the Old, Old Story: The Art of Narrative Preaching*, 67.

4. Step 1: Anticipation

1. Andy Stanley and Lane Jones, *Communicating for a Change: Seven Keys to Irresistible Communication* (Colorado Springs: Multnomah Books, 2006), ebook edition, chap. 15.

2. Eugene Lowry, *The Homiletical Plot: The Sermon as Narrative Art Form*, expanded ed. (Louisville: Westminster John Knox, 2001), ebook edition, section 1.

3. Al Tompkins, *Aim for the Heart: Write, Shoot, Report, and Produce for TV and Multimedia* (Washington, DC: CQ Press, 2012), ebook edition, chap. 4.

4. Eugene Lowry, *The Homiletical Plot: The Sermon as Narrative Art Form*, section 2.

5. I am grateful to Al Tompkins for the rubber band metaphor.

6. Blair Warren, *The One Sentence Persuasion Course* (Blair Warren, 2012), ebook edition, chap. 4.

7. Ibid.

8. William James, *Psychology: Briefer Course* (New York: Henry Holt and Company, 1892), 448.

5. Step 2: Grace

1. John Wesley, "The Means of Grace," *Sermons 1*, The Bicentennial Edition of the Works of John Wesley, ed. Albert C. Outler (Nashville: Abingdon Press, 1984), 1:376; General Rules of the Methodist Societies.

2. Rick Warren, *What on Earth Am I Here For?*, ex. ed. (Grand Rapids, MI: Zondervan, 2012), ebook edition, section 1.

3. I am grateful to Matt Keller for his insights on the story of Jacob. Matt Keller, *God of the Underdogs: When the Odds Are Against You, God Is For You* (Nashville: Nelson Books, 2013), chap. 3.

6. Step 3: Answer

1. Charley Reeb, *Mission Possible: Cycle B Sermons for Advent, Christmas, and Epiphany Based on the Gospel Texts* (Lima, OH: CSS Publishing Company, 2014), 62.

2. Charley Reeb, "The Secret," September 18, 2016, sermon, Day1, http://day1.org/7411-the_secret.

3. Rev. Sara Ofner-Seals' sermon "Rolling Away the Stone: An Easter Sermon on Mark 16" served as fodder for my point; see http://sara -fromthehill.blogspot.com/2012/04/rolling-away-stone-easter-sermon-on .html.

4. Roy H. Williams, *The Wizard of Ads: Turning Words into Magic and Dreamers into Millionaires* (Austin, TX: Bard Press, 1998), ebook edition, chap. 13.

5. Ben Decker and Kelly Decker, *Communicate to Influence: How to Inspire Your Audience to Action* (New York: McGraw Hill, 2015), ebook edition, chap. 5.

6. "Because every cigarette shortens your life, which moment are you willing to give away?," YouTube video, 0:18, from TobaccoFreeCA.com posted by "David Huddleston," November 5, 2013, https://www.youtube .com/watch?v=oXNTDFgQTg0; see also www.TobaccoFreeCA.com.

7. Step 4: Proclamation

1. Simon Sinek, "Start with Why: How Great Leaders Inspire Action," YouTube video, 18:01, from TEDx Puget Sound in 2009, posted by "TEDx Talks," September 28, 2009, https://www.youtube.com /watch?v=u4ZoJKF_VuA.

8. Step 5: Explosion

1. William L. Self, *Surviving the Stained-Glass Jungle* (Macon, GA: Mercer University Press, 2011), 79.

2. Charley Reeb, "Romans 6:3-11" in *Feasting on the Word: Preaching the Revised Common Lectionary, Year C, Vol. 2,* eds. David L. Bartlett and Barbara Brown Taylor (Louisville: Westminster John Knox Press, 2009), 347.

3. Quoted in Bob Kelly, *Worth Repeating: More Than 5,000 Classic and Contemporary Quotes* (Grand Rapids, MI: Kregel Publications, 2003), 263.

4. Michael Port, *Steal the Show* (New York: Houghton Mifflin Harcourt, 2015), ebook edition, chap. 11.

9. Putting It All Together

1. Charley Reeb, "The Secret," September 18, 2016, sermon, Day1, http://day1.org/7411-the_secret.

2. *The Shawshank Redemption*, DVD, directed by Frank Darabont (1994; Burbank, California: Warner Home Video, 2010).

3. I am grateful to Al Tompkins for this insight.

4. Lane Sebring, *Preaching Killer Sermons: How to Create and Deliver Messages That Captivate and Inspire* (Centreville, VA: Preaching Donkey, 2016), ebook edition, chap. 8.

5. Thom and Joan Schultz, *Why Nobody Wants to Go to Church Anymore: And How 4 Acts of Love Will Make Your Church Irresistible* (Loveland, CO: Group Publishing, 2013), 127.

6. Reg Grant and John Reed, *The Power Sermon: Countdown to Quality Messages for Maximum Impact* (Primedia eLaunch, 2013), ebook edition, chap. 11.

7. Nancy Duarte provides great insight into how effective sermons and speeches create emotional contrast. Nancy Duarte, *Resonate: Present Visual Stories That Transform Audiences* (Sunnyvale, CA: Duarte Press, 2012), ebook edition, chap. 6.

8. Ibid., chap. 2.

9. From an Advent preaching workshop led by Tom Long at St. Luke's UMC in Windermere, Florida in the early 2000s.

10. Clyde Fant, *Preaching for Today* (New York: Harper and Row, 1975), 118–22.

11. Grant and Reed, *The Power Sermon*, chap. 11.

12. Tom Long workshop at St. Luke's UMC in Windermere, Florida, in early 2000s.

Conclusion

1. O. Wesley Allen's book *Determining the Form* is a useful tool for experimenting with different forms of preaching; O. Wesley Allen, *Determining the Form: Structures for Preaching* (Minneapolis: Fortress Press, 2008).